THE BROADCASTER'S LEGAL GUIDE FOR CONDUCTING CONTESTS AND PROMOTIONS

James A. Albert, J.D.

© 1985 by Bonus Books, Inc., and James A. Albert, J.D.

Library of Congress Catalog Card Number
85-60744

International Standard Book Number:
0-933893-08-6

Bonus Books, Inc.
160 East Illinois Street
Chicago, Illinois 60611

Printed in the United States of America

CONTENTS

FOREWORD

In 1969, a radio station in Virginia advertised that the winner of a station promotion contest would win "the keys to a new Impala." The winner received as his prize a set of Impala car keys, but no car.

That example from Jim Albert's book shows why the Federal Communications Commission intrudes into the broadcasting business.

This book contains hundreds of other examples of faulty contests that have put unsuspecting broadcasters in jeopardy of a monetary penalty, short-term renewal, or worse, license revocation. Radio and television stations face these situations daily.

As you will see as you read, this book clearly illustrates how a broadcaster can stay out of contest and promotion trouble, and offers constructive advice on what to do if licensees find themselves in violation. *The Broadcaster's Legal Guide for Conducting Contests and Promotions* is a desk top reference. It is essential to the professional broadcaster, advertising agency, business, broadcast lawyer or anyone else who must understand the potential dangers in contests and promotions and how to present them legally.

The author uses common sense and focuses on problems from the local broadcaster's perspective. For example, once a violation occurs and the broadcaster is caught in a contest crisis, Albert provides some sage advice that alone is worth the price of the book:

- Be first to notify the FCC.
- Quickly investigate the allegations.

- Act decisively to punish wrongdoing.

- Take steps to eliminate recurrence.

Read this book and learn. I did. So will you.

Thomas E. Bolger
President & Chief Executive Officer
Forward Communications Corporation
Madison, WI

ACKNOWLEDGMENTS

I wish to recognize here some special people whose talents contributed to the preparation of this book.

Professor John Lytle of the Drake University School of Journalism and Mass Communication and a former radio broadcaster competently edited these chapters. Karla Westberg, faculty secretary at the Drake University Law School, painstakingly and flawlessly typed the early drafts and the final manuscript. Michael Clarizio, now an assistant state's attorney in Cook County, Illinois, who as a third-year law student at Drake served as my research assistant, briefed and analyzed several of the cases discussed in chapters 16 and 17. And Thomas Bolger, president and chief operating officer of Forward Communications Corporation and a former National Association of Broadcasters officer, wrote the thoughtful and articulate foreword to the book.

Also on this list are my parents, Mr. and Mrs. Richard Albert, and my teenaged sons, Brian and Brad Albert. They do their part to support the broadcasters this book is designed to help by listening to as much radio and watching as much television as any four other people in America, and still have the time to be the best family with which anyone could be blessed.

I also want to particularly thank the hundreds of enthusiastic broadcast law students with whom I've worked in my classes at the University of South Dakota and at the Drake Law School.

Too, Dean Richard Calkins of Drake gave me the chance, Associate Dean Edward Hayes gave me a class schedule which facilitated this research, my friends on the faculty gave me the lift of collegiality and the law librarians gave me help all along the way.

And Judge Jack R. Miller of the United States Court of Appeals for the Federal Circuit really started it all by recommending a young kid fresh out of law school to the FCC in Washington as a new staff attorney in 1976.

It is to all of these people and the radio and television broadcasters throughout the country that this book is dedicated.

James A. Albert, J.D.

CHAPTER 1

The Popularity of Station Contests

For many radio stations across the country, contests are as integral to their programming as music, news or commercials. In fact, the *Radio Promotion Handbook*—an industry guide—acknowledges that "[t]he top 40 and other popular music stations have demonstrated that it is best to have at least one contest on the air at all times."[1] Today, radio stations representing every conceivable format—from easy listening to hard rock—regularly air contests.

TV stations, too, frequently air contests, from popular dialing-for-dollars programs during afternoon movies to highly-publicized trivia contests which highlight certain of their own programs. Contests are significant tools of local TV station promotion departments.

History suggests that the burgeoning popularity of television in the early 1950s in fact forced local radio programmers to compete for audiences through new formats of music and news and to attempt to breathe new vitality into radio by broadcasting contests. Thirty years later, contests remain popular because they deliver audiences and improve ratings. The average listener enjoys the excitement and spontaneity when a disc jockey places a "Cash Call" for a jackpot of money or offers lucky dollars for correctly identifying a mystery sound.

Contests work for broadcasters and the success stories are legion.

Top Fifty Major Markets

When Los Angeles station KFWB switched its format to popular music in 1955, thousands of balloons were pushed from the windows of downtown office buildings. One of every five balloons carried a one or fifty dollar bill. As Claude Hall, the radio-TV editor for *Billboard* magazine recalls:

> Traffic was tied up for hours over about 200 square miles. But everyone quickly knew about rock 'n' roll music on KFWB. It became the No. 1 station in Los Angeles as fast as people could switch radio dials.[2]

When Chicago's WMAQ switched to a country music format in January of 1975, it launched contests that continued at least nine years. The slogan "WMAQ Is Gonna Make You Rich" was repeated so often each day it became the station's broadcasting signature. By October, 1982 "millions of dollars" had been won by listeners, and all of it "made a big impact in Chicago."[3]

Across town, WLS responded with its own high-stakes "Music Radio Game," which first aired in 1977. Within the next few years, WLS awarded thirty Hawaiian vacations (which included air fare, lodging and meals), twenty Chevrolet automobiles, thirty-one motorcycles, a home, one hundred vacations to Disney World and $40,000 worth of stereo equipment.[4]

Chicago's WFYR sponsored a St. Patrick's Day contest for ten days in 1983 in which listeners could win a trip to Ireland. Contestants telephoned the station with their favorite Irish jokes and disc jockeys selected the best. Earlier, 75,000 Chicagoans had entered FYR's contest which asked listeners to write down and send in the names of any three songs played by the station during any fifteen-minute period during the day. The listener whose card was drawn at random from the sea of entries received $10,000 in cash.[5]

Columbus, Ohio, television station WBNS-TV aired a "Great Moments Trivia Contest" in 1983 which challenged viewers to answer TV trivia questions about popular WBNS and CBS programs. Questions ranged from "On Falcon Crest, what is the family business?" to "Tom Selleck plays a cool, good-looking private investigator on what CBS show?" The contestants who correctly answered the forty-three total questions were declared winners. Hundreds of prizes were given away, including a color television.[6]

The last television episode of "M*A*S*H" in the spring of 1983 inspired numerous local station contests and promotions. Prizes were often awarded for the costumes best simulating official "M*A*S*H" attire. Among those stations sponsoring such "M*A*S*H" events were WRIF and WKBD-TV (Detroit), WGAR and WJKW-TV (Cleveland), KMEL (San Francisco), WPLR (New Haven, CT), WIOD (Miami), WEHT-TV (Evansville, IN), WFSB (Hartford, CT), WRQX (Washington, DC), WSTO (Owensboro, KY), and WAAF (Boston).[7]

In Cleveland, WGAR conducted an "Ugly Car Contest" in which listeners submitted photographs of their clunkers. The owner of the ugliest car was declared the winner and awarded a CB radio and four new tires. Runners up received cases of motor oil.[8]

The 1983 "Cupid Contest" of Detroit's WXYZ-TV invited

married couples to submit, in fifty words or less, their formulas for keeping romance fresh in their marriages. The winners were lavished with candlelight dinners, shows, chauffeured limousine service, a variety of personal gifts, and a weekend in the posh honeymoon suite of an area hotel.[9]

For correctly identifying sixteen various sounds made by a jeep, listeners of WCAU-AM in Philadelphia could win a new 1983 AMC Jeep and a weekend in the Poconos. The jeep sounds tape was played throughout the day and contestants were required to sort out the sounds and send their guesses in writing to the station.[10]

WCCO-FM in Minneapolis offered listeners a chance to win $25,000 in a continuing contest which showcased CCO's mostly-music format. If any listener caught the station playing fewer than four songs in a row, that person would win $25,000 on the spot. As of January of 1983, there had been three separate winners.[11]

A "Star Trek Marathon Contest" was aired by WTXX-TV in Hartford, Connecticut, as a part of the station's twenty-six-hour "Star Trek" extravaganza which aired at 8:00 p.m. one Friday night and ran straight through until 10:00 p.m. Saturday. Viewers could pick up contest cards at area 7-Eleven stores and Mazda dealers—the co-sponsors of the twenty-six-hour programming block. There were twenty-six questions on the trivia contest cards with one question based on each episode broadcast. More than 2,500 viewers submitted entries and the winner won a trip to Walt Disney World for four people.[12]

Second Fifty Major Markets

KFMB-FM, San Diego, offered listeners a chance to win $20,000 if they were the 100th caller after three Supremes, Eagles and Fleetwood Mac hits were played in a certain order.[13]

KSO, at 146 on the AM band in Des Moines, Iowa, sponsored a brief contest prior to the NCAA Regional semi-final basketball game in March of 1983. Two courtside tickets to the Iowa Hawkeyes-Villanova Wildcats championship game were to be awarded to the 146th caller. The contest was announced on the air at 7:30 a.m. the day before the game and within fifteen minutes, 50,000 listeners telephoned the station hoping to win the tickets.[14]

The granddaddy of contests—the venerable "Cash Call"— where contestants send in post cards and then wait to be called while keeping track of a changing amount of money in the jackpot, has done the job for Rochester, New York, station WPXY. Explains Promotion Director Louis Ignatti, "Monthly ratings increase dramatically"[15] when contests are aired.

Portland, Maine's WPOR-FM noted "enthusiastic audience participation"[16] in the eighteen contests it ran in the 1982–1983 year. The most successful game—"Match 'n Win"—placed thousands of game boards printed with the station's logo into area homes. Sponsoring businesses paid $1,000 each for spot packages and also donated $100 prizes for the winners.

WDBO in Orlando, Florida broadcasts thirty contests a year. The one that recently increased station visibility was the "Bumper Sticker Contest." Colorful WDBO bumper stickers were made available to area motorists. Those drivers who adorned their cars with them became eligible to win when a spotter driving a station car prowled the streets of Orlando and pulled them over.[17]

Orlando competitor WBJW-FM, with a contemporary hit format, found that the most effective contests were those that tied in with the music the station played. Their 1983 Beatles song contest, for instance, offered $10,000 to the third listener who called the station after three Beatles hits in a row were played. Program Director Garry Mitchell rated that contest a success because it encouraged sampling of the station by new listeners and continued listening by the established audience.[18]

Roanoke, Virginia's WTOY aired twenty-five contests during a twelve-month period in 1982–1983. "The Silver Dollar Man" giveaway generated the most public attention, as clues were broadcast hourly as to the identity of TOY's Silver Dollar Man. The first listener to correctly guess who he was and confront him on the street with the greeting "[A]re you the WTOY Silver Dollar Man?" won 100 silver dollars. By the end of the contest run, ten listeners had solved the mystery and each walked away with $100. As Operations Manager Scot Morris analyzed it: "I don't think people listen to a station just because of the particular contest, but it keeps interest up in the community and keeps people talking about the station."[19]

Smaller Markets

In 1982, Springfield, Missouri, stations KTTS-AM and FM offered listeners the chance to win a brand-new pickup truck loaded with Mountain Dew in a modified treasure hunt. To win, contestants had to find the fourteen locations in town where the station had placed official contest posters. Enthusiastic about such promotions, Program Manager Bob Rose summed up his experience with them: "[t]he success of our contests is manifest in the strong position KTTS holds in the market as demonstrated by the Arbitron [ratings]. . . ."[20]

Grand Forks, North Dakota, station KKXL-AM is adult contemporary and KKXL-FM is top 40. In the 1982–1983 year, the two stations ran ten contests. Explains XL's Don Nordine: "[C]ontesting is only done to keep a certain level of excitement on each station."[21]

KMMJ in Grand Island, Nebraska, aired nine contests in 1982–1983. The station reports that the most popular have challenged the listeners—for instance the "KMMJ Weather Game," in which contestants were asked various questions about weather and meteorology.[22]

On the other hand, "simple and easy participation"[23] has been the key at adult contemporary KSMX in Fort Dodge, Iowa, which ran twelve contests in a twelve-month period during 1982 and 1983. The most successful was the "92 Button Contest" where listeners would pick up a 92 button at various participating retailers, wear it on their coat lapel around town, and be awarded from $9.20 to $92.00 instantly on the spot if approached by station personnel. General Manager Thomas Carmody is high on contests because they create "good will and loyalty"[24] for the station.

In Joplin, Missouri, KMBH-AM and KKUZ-FM sponsored a "Sweet Ole Boss Contest" in which listeners were asked to send in the name of their boss on company letterhead and explain why he or she should be chosen "S.O.B." of the week. The AM side is modern country and the FM is adult contemporary. The station's general manager, Gary Exline, reports that most contests "have been very effective, especially from the standpoint of generating sales revenue."[25] And that's certainly not a bad standpoint, Gary.

But not every contest is a station's deliverance. When illegally operated, some have become a station's deathknell.

1. W. Peck, *Radio Promotion Handbook,* p. 11, (1968).

2. C. Hall, *The Business of Radio Programming,* p. 135, (1977).

3. Telephone interview with Stephen Krasula, Promotions Department, WMAQ Radio, Chicago, IL (October 7, 1982).

4. C. Hall, *The Business of Radio Programming, supra* note 2, p. 144.

5. *Broadcasters Promotion Association, Inc., Newsletter,* April, 1983, p. 13.

6. *Ibid.,* p. 21.

7. *Ibid.,* p. 9–10

8. *Broadcasters Promotion Association, Inc., Newsletter,* March, 1983, p. 10.

9. *Ibid.,* p. 9.

10. *Ibid.,* p. 15.

11. *Broadcasters Promotion Association, Inc., Newsletter,* February, 1983, p. 14.

12. *Ibid.*

13. *Broadcasters Promotion Association, Inc., Newsletter,* April, 1983, p. 20.

14. "Hawk Fans Swamp KSO Phones in Ticket Contest," *The Des Moines Register,* March 25, 1983, p. 1-M, col. 1.

15. Response to station contest questionnaire submitted September 14, 1983, by Louis Ignatti, Promotion Director, WPXY Radio, Rochester, N.Y.

16. Response to station contest questionnaire submitted September 12, 1983, by Thomas Hennessey, Operations Manager, WPOR-FM Radio, Portland, Maine.

17. Response to station contest questionnaire submitted September 16, 1983, by Bob Adams, Operations Manager, WDBO Radio, Orlando, Fla.

18. Response to station contest questionnaire submitted September 13, 1983, by Garry Mitchell, Program Director, WBJW-FM Radio, Orlando, Fla.

19. Response to station contest questionnaire submitted September 7, 1983, by Scot D. Morris, Operations Manager, WTOY Radio, Roanoke, Va.

20. Response to station contest questionnaire submitted June 13, 1983, by Bob Rose, Program Manager, KTTS Radio, Springfield, Mo.

21. Response to station contest questionnaire submitted June 15, 1983, by Don Nordine, KKXL Radio, Grand Forks, N. Dak.

22. Response to station contest questionnaire submitted June 10, 1983, by Dan Arrasmith, Program Director, KMMJ Radio, Grand Island, Nebr.

23. Response to station contest questionnaire submitted June 9, 1983, by Thomas Carmody, General Manager, KSMX Radio, Fort Dodge, Iowa.

24. *Ibid.*

25. Response to station contest questionnaire submitted June 9, 1983, by Gary Exline, General Manager, WMBH-AM and KKUZ-FM, Joplin, MO.

CHAPTER 2

The Contest that Capsized a Local Station

While contests are enthusiastically aired by broadcast stations because of the listeners they quickly attract, stations must be as careful with contests as laboratory scientists are with vials of nitroglycerin. One major misstep in its operation of a contest and a station's license can be revoked by the federal government. It has happened several times before.

KIKX, TUCSON

The highest-rated radio station in Tucson, KIKX, had teenagers tuning to its rock format and its often outrageous and rowdy disc jockeys. Locked in a heated ratings battle with its competitors in January of 1974, KIKX concocted a promotion involving popular disc jockey "Crazy Man" Craig.

The station announced to a stunned audience that Craig (real name: Arthur Gopen) had been "kidnapped" from the site of a remote broadcast. KIKX aired a fabricated police report of the abduction and asked listeners to call the station or Tucson police with any clues regarding the disappearance.

The thrust of the contest was that Craig would immediately fly to Miami. On his return to Tucson, he would telephone the station from several locations, providing clues as to his whereabouts. The listener who correctly guessed the route he was taking back to Tucson would win the contest.[1]

But the false news reports of Craig's kidnapping so sparked the interest of local residents that they flooded police telephone lines with inquiries about Craig's safety. KIKX sensed a winning theme and quickly decided to "hype" the abduction. In fact, the part of the contest involving guessing his location never materialized.

The Tucson Police Department, knowing the event was fabricated and having its phone lines jammed with concerned listeners, ordered KIKX to "knock it off."[2] The station responded by increasing the pitch. It added reports of "search parties" and the sighting of the kidnap car.

Tucson's KGUN-TV was first on the air with the truth when it reported the whole "kidnapping as a hoax."[3] But KIKX swiftly broadcast a response which denied the hoax and pleaded for listeners with helpful information to come forward.

The station's general manager, sales manager and program director continued the ruse for four days. Then it was abruptly terminated on the advice of the station's attorney when station owner John Walton suddenly learned of the truth. Walton, an absentee owner who also controlled eight other radio and TV stations in Texas, California and New Mexico, then went on the air to admit the hoax and aplogize to the KIKX listeners. It was too late.

Enter the FCC

After six years of hearings and delays, the Federal Communications Commission (FCC) revoked the station's license in 1980 for the "cynical hoax, which needlessly shocked KIKX's listening audience and interfered with police operations by tying up their telephone lines."[4]

Walton protested that he was blameless since he was not personally involved in the incident and because he had adopted a station policy forbidding contest deceptions and improprieties.

The FCC reasoned that Walton could be held responsible for the acts of his employees through an application of a time-honored legal doctrine *(respondeat superior)* which places liability on an employer for the misdeeds of his employees. Also, the agency faulted KIKX contest policies as "more matters of form than substance"[5] since the personnel involved in the hoax had never seen them. The government concluded they remained policies on paper and not in practice.

The Commission sharply criticized Walton for failing to adequately supervise his KIKX employees and thus not exercising "the degree of care expected of Commission licensees."[6]

In May of 1982, the U.S. Court of Appeals for the District of Columbia Circuit affirmed the FCC's decision.[7] And on July 18, 1982, KIKX—which for thirty-six years had broadcast at 580 on the AM dial—played "The Last Cowboy Song" by Ed Bruce and went silent.[8]

The Audience Reacts

The FCC's stern action ignited a drumfire of protest in Arizona.

Station attorney Lester Spillane complained:

> I have been practicing communication law for 40 years . . .
> and this is one of the worst decisions I have ever seen.[9]

The *Arizona Daily Star*'s media columnist, David Hatfield, agreed when he wrote:

> I suppose some Federal Communications Commission
> bureaucrats, past and present, are gloating this week be-
> cause they succeeded in destroying a perfectly good radio
> station.
>   By killing off a radio station, the FCC has denied South-
> ern Arizonians another choice in its listening.[10]

Public sentiment was reflected in letters to the *Arizona Daily Star*. One local resident lamented:

> My family enjoyed listening to the station, and I am sure I
> speak for a lot of other fans when I say I can't see where
> penalizing those [current] employees for someone else's
> [the former disc jockeys and managers] wrongdoing is go-
> ing to accomplish anything—except make the unemploy-
> ment lines a little longer.[11]

Tucson Citizen columnist Jeff Smith railed that the FCC had overreacted and that the 1974 misconduct "never deserved the punishment it brought down on the station . . . or on Tucson radio listeners."[12]

He wrote that "[s]eventeen people who had absolutely noth-ing to do with the hoax [none of the current employees had been with the station in 1974] are out of work and on the street . . . because the FCC couldn't find humor or forgiveness in the situa-tion."[13]

Characterizing the incident as a joke which "grew from a harmless promotional contest into a major legal hassle,"[14] Smith assessed the impact of the FCC's decision on Tucson: "[It] has cost the station owners as much as a quarter of a million dollars in legal fees, has cost the Tucson radio audience a friendly voice, and, of course, has cost the aforementioned seventeen innocents their livelihoods."[15]

Crisply voicing the disapproval of many Tucson residents, columnist Smith concluded: "I think the FCC and the U.S. Court of Appeals in Washington are a bunch of shorthorns for acting as they have."[16]

The Commission has been called worse. Although often inviting local castigation for its regulation, insuring the honesty and integrity of radio and television station contests is a statutory responsibility of the Federal Communications Commission. In fact, federal regulation of broadcast contests was demanded by the public in the wake of the national quiz show scandals of the 1950s.

NOTES/2

1. D. Hatfield, ''What's FCC Done for Our Interests?'' *The Arizona Daily Star,* July 21, 1982, p. 2-D, col. 7.

2. *Walton Broadcasting, Inc.,* 78 F.C.C.2d 857, 860 (1980).

3. *Ibid.*

4. *Ibid.,* 866.

5. *Ibid.,* 865.

6. *Ibid.,* 867.

7. *Walton Broadcasting, Inc. v. Federal Communications Commission,* 679 F.2d 263 (D.C. Cir. 1982).

8. D. Hatfield, ''KIKX Ends Battle to Stay on Air, Plays Its Last Country Tune,'' *The Arizona Daily Star,* July 19, 1982, p. 1, col. 1.

9. S. Stern, ''KIKX Not Going Off the Air Despite FCC License Denial,'' *The Arizona Daily Star,* December 17, 1980, p. 8-D, col. 1.

10. D. Hatfield, *supra* note 1.

11. D. Hatfield, ''KIKX Affair Has Many Facets,'' *The Arizona Daily Star,* August 22, 1982, p. 8-L, col. 2.

12. J Smith, ''KIKX Ax Falls on Innocent Necks,'' *Tucson Citizen,* July 21, 1982, p. 11-B, col. 2.

13. *Ibid.* at col. 3.

14. *Ibid.*

15. *Ibid.*

16. *Ibid.*

CHAPTER 3

The Quiz Show Scandals of the 1950s

The glittering network quiz shows of the 1950s truly fascinated the nation and were the most popular programs on the air. Yet, the history of quiz shows constitutes a dark chapter in the annals of broadcasting; and one which strongly impacts on today's station contests.

"Twenty-One," which premiered on network television in 1956, was one of the most popular prime-time programs in television history.[1] It joined a galaxy of other fashionable TV quiz shows that included "The $64,000 Question," "The $64,000 Challenge," "Dotto," "The Big Surprise," "Tic Tac Dough," and "High Finance."

TV quizzes became a significant part of our culture as millions of Americans tuned their black and white sets to the likes of celebrities Vincent Price, Edward G. Robinson, and twenty-eight year old boxing expert Dr. Joyce Brothers. And thousands of ordinary citizens like shoemaker Gino Prato and a variety of housewives, policemen, and teachers fiercely competed for tens of thousands of dollars on each show.[2]

The set of "Twenty-One," emblazoned with rather sizable "Geritol" tradenames to honor the show's sole sponsor, featured a lighted isolation booth for each contestant to stand in as he or she labored to answer questions on topics from history to chemistry.

Typical "Twenty-One" questions asked contestants to explain the process of photosynthesis, to identify the three main Balearic Islands, and to name "the Republican vice-presidential candidate who died before Election Day in 1912."[3] (It was James S. Sherman).

U.S. Supreme Court Justice William O. Douglas was even recruited to draft a question which was used on "The Big Surprise."[4]

The sound-proof booths insulated the contestants from any untimely help from their friends in the studio audience and from the pervasive "thinking music," played while they attempted to dredge the answers from their memories. Each contestant wore headphones, appeared businesslike, and displayed scholarly seriousness in his or her responses to the often erudite questions which involved such big stakes for each night's winner.

When contestant Charles Van Doren won $129,000 on "Twenty-One," *Time* magazine elevated him to posterity and certain prominence by adorning its cover with his visage, accompanied by the legends "Quiz Champ Van Doren" and "Brains v. Dollars on TV."[5]

Van Doren, an English professor at Columbia University, went on to win $143,000 before being toppled by opponent Vivienne Nearing, a lawyer.

During its first year on the air (1955–1956), "The $64,000 Question" awarded ten Cadillacs and $648,000 in cash to winning contestants.[6] By the end of 1957, 175 mink coats had been won on "The Big Payoff."

It appeared, at least, that the money was being well-earned by the earnest scholars who sweated in those isolation booths, tortured by exceedingly difficult questions. The *New York Times* called these people "limited eggheads" who were well on their way to becoming national heroes.[7]

A twenty-eight-year old Marine became one of the few contestants to win all $64,000 on "The $64,000 Question" when he correctly answered a question about what King George VI had eaten for dinner the night of March 21, 1939.[8]. Elfrida Von Nardroff, a thirty-two-year old contestant on "Twenty-One," pushed her winnings to $146,000 by knowing the name of the prime minister who served England in 1721, his party, the king then on the throne and the royal family to which the king belonged. (Robert Walpole, Whig, King George I, Hanover).[9]

Robert Strom, a ten-year-old grade school student, captivated the public when he won $160,000 on "The $64,000 Question." And Theodore Nadler, a government clerk whose job paid only seventy dollars a week, became a popular winner as he amassed $152,000 on "The $64,000 Challenge."[10]

The national television audience loved it. One 1955 broadcast of "The $64,000 Question" attracted a viewing audience of more than 55 million people—a television milestone.[11] By 1956, that program had become the most popular and highly-rated TV show in the country.[12] On one evening during the 1956–1957 season, 89 percent of all television sets in use in the nation were tuned to that show.[13]

A quiz show mania swept the country. The three major television networks responded to the mass popularity of the quizzes by devoting seventy-five half hour periods each week to that type of program during 1957.[14]

The viewing public's appetite for quiz shows seemed insatiable. In the summer of 1958 alone, the networks unleashed ten new quiz programs. Among them was the flashy "Dotto," the challenge of which was to connect dots by correctly answering questions and in so doing guess the identity of a famous personality whose caricature was outlined by the dots. These "Dotto" puzzle faces ranged from Napoleon to Gabby Hayes.

"Dotto" was such a hit that it aired on two rival networks at the same time: a daytime version on CBS and a Tuesday night edition on NBC.[15]

But the real long-term significance of "Dotto" was that it was rigged; and a contestant who found out about it later told the world. Other contestants from other quiz shows then came forward with similar testimony and a national scandal exploded into front page banner headlines of the country's major newspapers.[16]

It was one Edward Hilgemeier, Jr., in fact a stand-by contestant who never did play "Dotto" on the air, who accidentally found another contestant's notes backstage. It was obvious that the notes included answers to the questions that were asked during the program. It was clear the contestant had been given the answers and that the show had been fixed. But before any local clean government committees start erecting Hilgeimeier statues, note parenthetically that his silence was first purchased for $1,500 by the producers and he did not blow the whistle. It was only later in 1958, upon learning that another contestant had been paid a healthier $4,000 to keep the same secret, that Hilgemeier's outrage erupted and he contacted the FCC.[17]

A New York housewife who had won $1,500 in four days on "Dotto" told *Time* magazine:

> Each morning, before the show goes on, each contestant sees a producer. He says something like . . . "Who holds the record for home runs? You know—Babe Ruth." Then he'll say: "How would you recognize David Nizen?" Sure enough, when the dots fill in, there's David Niven.[18]

The cat was out of the bag. "Dotto" was immediately dumped by NBC and CBS and the broadcast industry braced itself for a public relations bloodbath as other former contestants began to tell their own stories.

Congressional Investigation

The House Legislative Oversight Subcommittee conducted hearings in 1959 into the quiz show scandals. Of 152 witnesses in twenty-one days, the testimony that electrified the country came when the vaulted Van Doren himself shocked Congressmen on November 2, 1959, when he told them that each of his fourteen appearances on "Twenty-One" had been rigged. Testified Van Doren: "I was involved . . . in a deception."[19] He explained that he had been supplied with answers in advance and had even been coached to stammer and act as if he couldn't quite remember the answer until just before the time limit expired.

Daniel Enright, "Twenty-One's" producer, admitted providing answers to several contestants in advance of airtime; and that fully one half of their programs were fixed. He also acknowledged coaching them on acting techniques to enhance their performances.[20]

Popular band leader Xavier Cugat, who had appeared as a contestant on "The $64,000 Challenge" three times, testified at the Congressional hearing that he had been given the answers before each of the three shows.[21]

Admitted "Twenty-One" contestant Herbert Stempel: "I was told by the producers . . . to purposely lose to Van Doren."[22]

New York City Grand Jury Probe

The Congressional hearings of 1959 had been preceded by a vigorous New York inquiry. New York City District Attorney

Frank S. Hogan launched a powerful grand jury investigation of the scandal in the spring of 1958. The D.A. later concluded that the evidence established "a national fraud whereby television quiz shows have been constantly misrepresented to millions of citizens as honest tests of the contestants' knowledge and skill."[23]

During the course of the grand jury's probe, the extent of the rigging became clear. It was even revealed that "$64,000 Challenge" staffers had given the Rev. Charles E. Jackson, a contestant from Tullahoma, TN, the answer to a question before the show on which he appeared. Rev. Jackson won $4,000 on that program and had earlier winnings of $16,000 on "The $64,000 Question."[24]

The New York grand jury's investigation moved forward for two-and-a-half years. Much of the evidence it gathered was turned over to Congressional investigators who relied heavily upon it in their own hearings.

But in the final analysis, the Congressional response was to amend the Communications Act to make quiz and contest improprieties unlawful. New York's response was more direct: it arrested many of the quiz show celebrities. For lying to the grand jury when they denied any quiz show rigging during their early grand jury testimony, several contestants were indicated for perjury.

Those arrested in October of 1960 in New York City included "Twenty-One" contestants Charles Van Doren, Elfrida Von Nardroff, Hank Bloomgarden, Vivienne Nearing, Paul Bain, David Mayer, and Ruth Miller.

"Tic Tac Dough" participants booked at the New York police station were Mrs. Henrietta Dudley, Richard Klein, Joseph Rosner, Mrs. Patricia Sullivan, Dr. Michael Truppin, Morton Harelik, Timothy Horan, Mrs. Patricia Nance, and Mrs. Ruth Klein.[25]

The Nation Reacts

The country was jolted by the news. President Eisenhower expressed the prevailing outrage when he criticized the deception and rigging as a "terrible thing to do to the American people."[26] "Today" show host Dave Garroway actually cried on the air upon hearing the news.[27]

The quiz programs implicated in the scandals were unceremoniously axed by the networks, and sponsors scrambled to save their reputations from taint.

But the quiz show scandals of the 1950s still impact on broadcasters today because of the legislation the scandals generated. The relevance of flashy, $64,000 big money network quiz shows of 1958 to today's twenty-five dollar "Cash Call Jackpot" of a local radio station licensed to a town of 10,000 people is that the laws the Congress enacted to curb future quiz show rigging also make certain contest conduct illegal. The Congress speaks of quiz shows and promotional contests simultaneously.

Congress responded to the scandal by amending the Communications Act of 1934 to include Section 509 which makes unlawful various quiz and contest improprieties.[28] The FCC reacted by increasing its scrutiny of broadcast quizzes and on-the-air contests; and later, adopting its own contest rules and regulations.[29]

Disc jockeys and TV hosts in studios across the country today —hamstrung and strictly limited by the federal contest laws now on the books—can connect the dots and quickly identify the caricature of . . . Professor Charles Van Doren. Today's contest headaches are the legacy of the quiz show scandal headlines of the 1950s.

1. J. Fireman, *The Ultimate Television Book* p. 91 (1977).

2. *Ibid.*, pp. 89–93.

3. "The Wizard of Quiz," *Time*, February 11, 1957, p. 44.

4. "The Week in Review," *Time*, November 7, 1955, p. 77.

5. *Time*, February 11, 1957.

6. "The Busy Air," *Time*, June 18, 1956, p. 84.

7. G. Cottler, "The Question About Quiz Shows," *The New York Times*, December 1, 1957, Sect. 6, p. 94, col. 2.

8. "The Week in Review," *Time*, September 26, 1955, p. 57.

9. "TV & Radio," *Time*, May 12, 1958, p. 70.

10. "The $60 Million Question," *Time*, April 22, 1957, p. 78.

11. J. Fireman, *supra* note 1, p. 91.

12. "The Busy Air," *Time*, June 18, 1956, p. 84.

13. G. Cottler, "The Question About Quiz Shows," *supra*, note 7, p. 93, col. 3.

14. *Ibid.*, p. 90, col. 2.

15. "Television and Radio," *Time*, August 11, 1958, p. 36.

16. Those newspapers included the *Chicago Tribune, Pittsburgh Post-Gazette, Los Angeles Mirror News, The Boston Globe* and *New York World-Telegram*. See "A Sad End To the Quiz Era," *Broadcasting*, November 9, 1959, p. 39.

17. T. Brooks & E. Marsh, *The Complete Directory To Prime Time Network TV Shows* pp. 169–170 (1979).

18. "Scandal of the Quizzes," *Time*, September 1, 1958, p. 38.

19. "A Sad Ending to the Quiz Era," *supra* n. 16.

20. *Ibid.,* p. 42.

21. *Ibid.,* p. 44.

22. J. Fireman, *supra* note 1, p. 92.

23. M. Murphy, "Hogan Asks Judge to Air TV Findings," *The New York Times,* July 14, 1959, p. 1, col. 7.

24. "Minister Says Quiz Gave Him TV Reply," *The New York Times,* September 7, 1958, p. 86, col. 1. Also see "A Sad Ending to the Quiz Era," *supra* note 16, p. 44.

25. "Footnote to a Fraud," *Broadcasting,* October 24, 1960, p. 60.

26. J. Fireman, *supra,* note 1, p. 93.

27. *Ibid.*

28. House Comm. on Interstate and Foreign Commerce, *Communications Act Amendments,* 1960, H. R. Rep No. 1800, 86th Cong., 2d Sess. (1960).

    See 47 U.S.C. § 509 (1982).

29. "FCC Outlines Law to Penalize All TV Quiz Riggers," *Advertising Age,* February 15, 1960, p. 2.

    See 47 C.F.R. § 73.1216 (1983).

CHAPTER 4

The Contest Laws Now on the Books

Three types of contest obligations are imposed on all broadcast stations: those contained in federal statutes enacted by the Congress; those promulgated by the FCC as standing rules and regulations of that agency; and those issued periodically by the FCC as public notices to the broadcast industry.

Regardless of whether the Congress or the FCC dictates an obligation in this area, it is the duty of the broadcaster to understand it and fully comply with it.

Federal Statutes

Section 509 of the Communications Act of 1934[1] makes it unlawful for any broadcaster to deceive the public by providing any "special and secret assistance"[2] to any contestant in any contest and in that way prearrange or predetermine its outcome. Even clarifying a contest clue given on the air for a listener who later calls the station would be considered "special assistance" because the clarification would not be available to all listeners. Stations should therefore avoid trying to accommodate individual contestants in that way or virtually any other way. This section also prohibits "any artifice or scheme"[3] on the part of the station to fix or rig a contest and thereby predetermine the winner or loser. For violating either of these provisions, an individual—a disc jockey, a TV host, a promotion director, a general manager or an owner—is subject to a maximum penalty of $10,-000 in fines and one year imprisonment.

Section 503(b)(1)(c) of the Act[4] imposes forfeiture liability on whichever person or corporate entity holds the FCC license for the broadcast station itself for airing a contest which violates Section 509. A daily fine of $2,000, with a maximum accumulation of $20,000, can be assessed.

Section 312(a)(4) of the Act[5] enpowers the FCC to revoke the license of any station which willfully or repeatedly violates any provision of the Communications Act, and that certainly includes Section 509. The FCC's licensing power must be respected because the licensing of broadcast stations is at the core of the FCC's mandate from Congress and forms the cutting edge of its jurisdiction.

No radio or television station can go on the air without a license from the FCC. Those licenses confer a limited, expiring five-year (for television) or seven-year (for radio) privilege to the license holder ("licensee") that can be renewed for subsequent terms only if the FCC determines the licensee's past service has been in the public interest.[6] Take note that the Commission has made it clear that stations which violate the contest laws breach their duty to operate in the public interest.

And, Section 312(a)(6)[7] expands the sanction of license revocation to cases involving violations of the U.S. Criminal Code provision which prohibits "any scheme or artifice to defraud . . . [by means of] radio or television."[8] It is, of course, quite conceivable that certain contests could defraud the public and trigger license revocation under this section.

FCC Rules and Regulations

The FCC is empowered to enact its own rules and regulations to carry out its regulatory functions.[9] Section 73.1216 of the Commission's published rules[10] details the various requirements the FCC imposes on its licensees which conduct or advertise contests.

The rule requires stations to:

> fully and accurately disclose the material terms of the contest, and . . . conduct the contest substantially as announced or advertised. No contest description shall be false, misleading or deceptive with respect to any material term.[11]

In published notes accompanying the rule, the FCC defines "contest" as an event where a prize is awarded to the public based on chance, skill or knowledge; and defines "material term" as information on such matters as how to enter, eligibility restrictions, entry deadlines, prizes, selection of winners, and tie-breaking procedures.

It must be emphasized—and etched in the mind of every person in radio or television who is involved in any way in a station's contests—that violation of this Commission regulation can result in revocation of the offending station's license.[12]

In complying with the rule requiring full disclosure of contest terms, good station practice would be to actually prepare a list of all the rules for each contest. The list should include:

1) the eligibility requirements;

2) nature and value of the prizes;

3) number of entries permitted;

4) how to enter;

5) the basis for determining the winners;

6) the dates of the contest; and,

7) tie-breaking procedures.

These rules should be written in plain, understandable language and be available to the public in printed form. A sample rules list will be found at the end of this chapter.

It is not necessary to disclose this full list of material terms each time a station promotes or runs a contest. Rather, two promotional cartridges should be prepared: one with all rules read in full; and the other, a brief functional promo, with only those rules most important to the particular contest briefly mentioned. The first cartridge need be played only occasionally during the contest. The other brief promo cartridge can then be utilized extensively.

If a station purchases newspaper advertising as part of a mix of media promotion of a contest, the full terms of the contest should be included in those newspaper ads which are large enough. Small teaser ads need not include any material terms.

Television promotion of contests should be conducted comparable to radio. Brief televised promos need not contain a full listing of terms, but one video announcement should be prepared and occasionally run which at least visually alerts viewers to all of the contest terms.

The promos detailing the contest terms need not be aired during any period of pre-contest hype. It is only when the contest is launched and the audience is told initially how to enter that the material terms must be disclosed.

With respect to reporting the "nature and value of the prizes," it is proper to list the normal retail price of any prize obtained for free by a station in exchange for advertising time.

If circumstances outside the control of the licensee necessitate changing a material term of the contest after it is underway, the licensee can avoid FCC punishment by prompt action. First, it must act reasonably and not disadvantage any contestants. Second, it must announce the changes immediately and conspicuously.

In the event a prize which was originally announced becomes unavailable, it is permissible to substitute one of equivalent value. To substitute prizes without incurring the wrath of the FCC, a station must act in good faith from the start of the contest in believing and asserting that the prize announced will be available at the close of the contest.[13]

FCC Public Notices

The FCC regularly issues public notices and policy statements to alert its licensees to avoid certain practices or adopt others. Such policy statements—when published in the "Federal Register" or "FCC Reports"—have the force of law.[14]

In 1960, the Commission adopted an omnibus programming policy statement that enumerated myriad obligations the agency expected its licensees to meet in their programming. The section on advertising and commercials noted the following:

> With respect to advertising material, the licensee has the additional responsibility to take all reasonable measures to eliminate any false, misleading or deceptive matter . . . This duty is personal to the licensee and may not be delegated.[15]

Later, the FCC elaborated on the responsibilities of its licensees regarding advertising in a 1969 Public Notice.

Maintaining that "the Commission has always held that a licensee's duty to protect the public from false, misleading or deceptive advertising is an important ingredient of his operation in the public interest,"[16] it explained:

> that licensee responsibility is not limited merely to a review of the advertising copy submitted for broadcast, but . . . [it must satisfy itself as to the advertiser's] ability to fulfill promises made to the public over the licensed facilities.[17]

In response to numerous complaints received from the public charging that several station contests, and particularly those of the treasure hunt genre, had resulted in private and public property damage, the FCC in 1966 adopted a Public Notice reproachful of such contests.

Recognizing that eager contestants searching for the "treasure" at times damaged parks, lawns, libraries and even museums as they "dug up the ground or ransacked"[18] those places, the Commission declared such contests would not be condoned. Of further concern to the FCC were reports that several of these contests had attracted large crowds which "blocked traffic, created disorder, and necessitated the diversion of police from other duties."[19]

The Public Notice emphasized that if contests generated such annoyances, a serious question would be raised "as to the sense of responsibility of the broadcast licensee involved,"[20] thus holding out the threat of a Commission inquiry into such a question during routine license renewal proceedings.

In 1974, the FCC published a vigorous and clear policy statement on contest integrity which underscored a licensee's contest responsibilities in narrow and specific detail.[21]

The Commission stated that certain contest conduct would automatically raise the question as to whether or not the licensee had met its statutory obligation to operate in the public interest.

That conduct included:

1. Disseminating false or misleading prize information;
2. Denying contestants a fair opportunity to win;
3. The failure of management to control and supervise the contest to avoid improprieties;
4. Failing to award the prizes announced;
5. Not awarding the prizes within a reasonable time;
6. Failing to fully explain contest rules;
7. Changing the rules without notifying the public;
8. Judging contest entries arbitrarily.

This detailed policy statement also required licensees to instruct their employees on legal contest procedures and to subsequently supervise those employees to insure that those instructions were followed.[22]

To emphasize the importance the Commission attached to adherence to these contest integrity responsibilities, the statement employed plain language threatening violations with license revocation. Warned the FCC: "In the future we will consider designation of a [license] renewal application for hearing . . . [when there exists] a pattern of repeated failure to conduct contests and promotions fairly or to advertise them truthfully."[23]

In fact, the violation of any of the different contest obligations discussed in this chapter can result in a variety of penalties. And the FCC has busied itself over the years meting out such punishment in contest cases.

SAMPLE STATION CONTEST FORM TO COMPLY WITH FCC RULE § 73.1216

WXYZ's Cash Call Jackpot

Contest Rules

Date Released

1. Any person over seventeen years of age can enter, except employees of the contest's sponsoring businesses and their families, employees of this station and their families, and persons who have won any prize in a WXYZ contest within the past six months. ("eligibility requirements")

2. Winners will receive all the money in the Cash Call Jackpot at the time they're called — from $10 to $1,000. ("nature and value of prizes")

3. Enter by sending a postcard with your name, address and telephone number to WXYZ, Anytown, U.S.A. Entries must be received by September 1, (insert year). ("how to enter")

4. Only one postcard per household, please. ("number of entries permitted")

5. The amount in each Jackpot will be announced at various times throughout the day; and the game will be played three times each day. A postcard will be drawn at random, and that person will be called on the air. The contestant will win the amount in the Jackpot if he or she correctly identifies exactly how much money is in that hour's Jackpot. ("basis for determining winner")

6. The contest will air from September 1 through October 1, (insert year). ("dates of contest")

7. No purchase necessary. (a phrase necessary to insure the contest will not be classified as an illegal lottery)

8. In the event of a tie, identical prizes will be awarded the winners. ("tie-breaking procedures") [This particular tie-breaking provision is essential in contests involving skills rather than breaking the tie by awarding the prize to the entry with the earliest postmark, for instance, because the introduction of that element of chance or luck by being the first to enter could result in categorizing the contest as an illegal lottery. See Chapter 16 for a further discussion of lotteries.]

(These contest rules should be typed and duplicated on station letterhead.)

1. 47 U.S.C. § 509 (1982).

2. *Ibid.*

3. *Ibid.*

4. 47 U.S.C. § 503(b)(1)(C) (1982).

5. 47 U.S.C. § 312(a)(4) (1982).

6. The FCC's licensing powers are enumerated in 47 U.S.C. §§ 301, 303, 307–312 (1982), and 47 C.F.R. §§ 73.3511, 73.3533, 73.3538, 73.3539, 73.3540, 73.3541, 73.3591, 73.3592, 73.3593, 73.3597, 73.3061, and 73.3605 (1983).

7. 47 U.S.C. § 312(a)(6) (1982).

8. 18 U.S.C. § 1343 (1982).

9. 47 U.S.C. §§ 154(i), 303(r) (1982). The FCC's rules and regulations are enumerated in 47 C.F.R. §§ 0.1 *et seq.* (1983).

10. 47 C.F.R. § 73.1216 (1983).

11. *Ibid.*

12. 47 U.S.C. § 312(a)(4) (1982).

13. See *Notice of Proposed Rulemaking,* 40 Fed. Reg. 26692, June 25, 1975; and *Licensee-Conducted Contests,* 60 FCC 2d 1072 (1976).

14. 47 C.F.R. §§ 0.445(d) and (e) (1983).

15. *En banc Programming Inquiry,* 44 FCC 2303, 2313 (1960).

16. *False, Misleading or Deceptive Advertising,* 40 FCC 125 (1961).

17. *Ibid.,* 126.

18. *Public Notice Re Contests and Promotions Which Adversely Affect the Public Interest,* 2 FCC 2d 464 (1966).

19.   *Ibid.*

20.   *Ibid.*

21.   *In Re Public Notice Concerning Failure of Broadcast Licensees to Conduct Contests Fairly*, 45 FCC 2d 1056 (1974).

22.   *Ibid.*, 1057.

23.   *Ibid.*

CHAPTER 5

The Contest Gauntlet—The FCC Procedures Which Stations Face

FCC procedures which form the various stages of Commission action on any contest allegation are illuminated from the perspective of the local broadcaster in this chapter. First, an overview of the role of the FCC and an analysis of its decision-making processes will be provided as background information.

An Introduction to Decision-making at the FCC

What Do Those Bureaucrats Do with Their Time, Anyway?

The Federal Communications Commission was created by Congress in 1934 . . . and it's been busy ever since. Its extensive responsibilities include regulating radio and television broadcasting, cable television, telephone and telegraph, communications satellites, CB radio, police radio and ship-to-shore communication.

Its agents patrol the highways of all fifty states in mobile vans boasting elaborate electronics equipment to monitor radio transmissions, its employees manage the Emergency Broadcast System as our country's nuclear attack alert mechanism, its scientists track futuristic satellites far above the earth, and its engineers even police garage door opener frequencies. Too, its attorneys regulate the heck out of radio and TV stations.

In all, there are 1,800 employees of the FCC. That's a relatively small number when one considers what that band of bureaucrats is responsible for overseeing: 1,000 local TV stations; 8,600 radio stations; 11,000 cable television systems; 33,-000 satellites, receivers, microwave bases and public land mobile units; 420,000 private radios abroad ships; 47,000 police radios; and millions of CB radio operators.[1]

But 350 of those FCC staffers spend their days regulating and licensing radio and television stations. And let's say you're a radio or television station owner or manager. What they do with their time to you or for you is the most relevant question when it comes to the government's communications responsibilities and its arsenal of manpower.

Why Are You Subject to Such Extensive Federal Regulation?

To put the whole thing into rather interesting historical perspective, it was broadcasters themselves who demanded federal regulation of their industry in the 1920's when no laws limited the activities of their competitors. Radio stations at that time would change frequencies at will, increase power and change their hours of operation. In one seven month period, 200 new stations went on the air using frequencies of their choice and often causing severe interference with the signals of existing stations.[2] Listeners were faced with chaos on their radio dials— they often couldn't receive clear, consistent signals of their favorite stations due to the confusion and spectrum jamming that ruled. The U.S. Supreme Court would later note that "[r]egulation of radio was therefore as vital to its development as traffic control was to the development of the automobile."[3]

The White House and Congress were responsive to the pleas of the broadcasters and the public; and the Federal Radio Act of 1927 became law. The federal government was in the business. And as the years wore on, the feds expanded their involvement in broadcasting. The Communications Act of 1934, which created the Federal Communications Commission remains the primary statutory framework within which stations must operate today. Amended throughout the decades, the Act empowers the FCC to license all radio and television stations in the country.

While broadcasters never objected to that type of traffic control, it was the whole array of obligations attendant to those licenses which Congress and the FCC imposed on broadcasters in return for the licenses which increasingly burdened and sometimes angered broadcasters. The strict contest rules are conspicuous among those obligations.

Why is it Difficult to Make Sense of FCC Decisions?

Many broadcasters complain that the FCC's contest rules are complex and confusing. And it's certainly true the laws could have been written with more clarity and precision. But they're no less clear than hundreds of other federal laws, rules and regulations that we endure—from the I.R.S. to O.S.H.A. to Social Security. Dealing with the federal government is rarely a simple matter.

Others maintain that even the FCC adjudications, decisions and policy statements which interpret and apply those contest laws to individual cases are often inconsistent and confounding. That simply can't be denied. Any honest review of all the FCC contest cases will reveal major inconsistencies—for example, obvious contest rigging in one case being punished by a short-term renewal or fine, and in another case apparently the same type of obvious unlawful rigging evoking only a letter of reprimand.

All of the decisions analyzed in this book do not fit neatly together, each a model of wisdom and reasoning and clarity. Every decision is not a tulip. There are a few weeds. Some stations got off with lighter punishment than others who committed similar contest offenses. While never fully satisfying to us, these differences and inconsistencies could be explained by factors which impact on each individual case: the credibility of the witnesses, the demeanor of the station management, the forcefulness of the evidence, the financial resources of the offending station and the competence of the attorneys on both sides—variables which we cannot appreciate as we read decisions years later but which a sitting Administrative Law Judge or FCC Commissioner could have picked up in an instant at a hearing.

Too, variations in FCC decisions could easily result from changes in Commission composition over the years. Each of the five (there used to be seven) FCC Commissioners is appointed by the President and confirmed by the Senate for staggered seven-year terms. Each assumes office with certain economic, political and regulatory philosophies often ingrained. Some Commissioners are more conservative, pro-broadcast industry and hesitant to regulate or penalize with vigor. Other more liberal members are often energetic in efforts to more fully regulate their radio and television licensees and more closely involve the government in licensee conduct. Obviously, shifts in Commission majorities from one philosophy to another often result in similar cases being decided differently over time. It can't be denied that a Commissioner's political and regulatory philosophy often dictates or influences how he or she will vote in a case and how stiff a penalty that Commissioner will be willing to impose for a contest violation.

Yet critics of the Commission's decision-making have been harsh in their censure of what they regard as haphazard adjudication of cases. Former FCC Chairman Newton Minow, upon leaving office, lamented that the Commission was "a quixotic world of undefined terms, private pressures and tools unsuited to the work."[4]

In a barrage of condemnation which was published in a 1973 *Yale Law Review* article, then Commissioner Nicholas Johnson expressed his outrage:

> On other matters [cases and policy decisions], the majority, presumably capable of comprehending the issues, reached bizarre conclusions or no conclusions at all.[5]

> [W]hen the Commission passes on matters beyond its "expertise" the results can be shocking.[6]

> [R]ational decision-making suffers [at the FCC].[7]

In sharp disagreement, former FCC Commissioner Kenneth Cox submitted a list of major Commission actions taken during a recent five-year period which consumed thirty-nine single-spaced pages. Included among those were headline-making FCC decisions on loud commercials, deceptive advertising, gambling, payola, plugola, the fairness doctrine, the personal attack rule, the compensation networks must pay their affiliates, broadcast ratings, a limit on the number of commercials that could be aired each hour, political candidates' use of radio and TV, and the development of UHF-TV stations. Cox concluded ''[W]e've handled an amazing array of problems . . . and . . . managed to get quite a bit done.''[8]

Logic and experience would dictate that the truth probably lies somewhere in between. This agency which umpires broadcasting in the country has made calls over the decades in contest cases, particularly, that have both incensed and satisfied broadcasters. In fact, for fifty years the FCC has labored to fulfill its statutory mandate of protecting the public interest through generally objective and painstaking decision-making. It has typically been judicious and fair, neither predisposed to any certain outcome of any particular case nor blindly allegiant to any interest group or influence. It has lumbered, albeit often with frustrating slowness, down the middle—calling the shots as it saw them. This referee is plainly overweight, encumbered by its encased bureaucracy and apparent inefficiency, but broadcasters every step of the way have received fair and impartial adjudication of their contest cases. The record shows the FCC and Administrative Law Judges have attempted in good faith to render the right decision in each particular case—the decision that the facts of the contest justified and the law required.

Once the FCC renders any initial or final decision in a contest case, it is made public by the Commission's Secretary in Washington, often distributed to the media, published in the bound volumes of the official FCC Reports which are sent to most libraries in the country,[9] and, if of general interest, reported by the industry trade press. Of course, if you're a party to the case, you'll receive a special copy of the decision as soon as it is available.

But what are the steps your case would follow from the moment the contest controversy develops to the date that final decision is released?

The Life of a Contest Case at the FCC

STEP 1:   The FCC is alerted to possible contest impropriety. A disgruntled contestant, a terminated employee or a broadcast competitor could write the FCC and charge that your "Cash Call Jackpot" was fixed. A challenger seeking to wrest your license might make such an allegation when it competes for that license at renewal time. A citizens' group could allege contest violations when you seek renewal of your license in order to stall your application. Or, a homeowner whose lawn has been trampled by your treasure hunt contest could indignantly protest to the FCC. Most typically, the FCC will consider such charges in conjunction with its review of your broadcast record at license renewal time.

STEP 2:   If the allegations are substantial, the staff of the FCC will investigate the matter. Commission employees assigned to the Mass Media Bureau have authority to investigate complaints from the public and pursue all issues related to license applications. Too, field enforcement agents of the FCC's Field Operations Bureau and its Enforcement Division are empowered to investigate specific stations' conduct in coordination with the legal staff in preparing cases for hearing.[10]

STEP 3:   As part of its investigation, the FCC staff may subpoena any of your papers or documents relating to the contest. Such a subpoena ordering you to produce these documents will be served by a United States Marshall or FCC representative.[11] Too, you could be interviewed by the FCC during this stage.

STEP 4:   The Mass Media Bureau will forward the results of its investigation to the five Commissioners of the agency. The Commissioners will then either drop the matter, being satisfied that the charges are groundless; or, decide to proceed against the station and order a full adjudication of the matter. If the latter decision is made, the following steps would be involved.[12]

STEP 5: The Commissioners will issue an order designating your case for hearing. You will be served with a "Notice of Designation for Hearing" alerting you to this fact and setting the time and place for hearing. The designation order will list the contest issues that the hearing will focus on, and detail the questions of fact and law that are to be decided. You must respond to this Notice within twenty days of receipt or lose your opportunity to be heard. It is imperative that you contact an attorney upon receipt of this Notice so that your right to appear is preserved. Your attorney will then respond with a written appearance and defend you at the hearing.[13] You could be ordered to give a deposition under oath during this time.

STEP 6: If the government is willing to spare you, an "out-of-court" settlement option may be explored and presented to you at the pre-hearing conference. The FCC's attorneys may ask at this time if you would be willing to negotiate such a settlement. These bargains typically include "consent agreements" between you and the FCC in which you accept some responsibility for the contest conduct.[14] Rarely has the FCC settled these contest controversies in this manner, however.

STEP 7: A hearing (comparable to a trial) will be held in Washington, D.C. at which an Administrative Law Judge (ALJ) presides. You will be represented by private counsel of your choice. The case against you will be prosecuted by an attorney from one of the trial staffs of the FCC. There will be no jury. The ALJ will be a specialist in broadcast law and will do most of the work at the trial. He or she will administer oaths, examine the witnesses, order the filing of legal briefs and conduct the bulk of the proceeding. The attorneys will be involved to the extent the case demands, with the government presenting its evidence and you introducing your evidence and any witnesses you select. As this is an administrative adjudication (the violation of most FCC contest rules is an administrative offense—not a criminal offense *per se* for which you could demand a jury trial), the ALJ alone will listen to all the evidence, review the pleadings and briefs and decide the case.[15]

STEP 8: The ALJ will issue an "Initial Decision." In it, the judge will either find you violated a contest rule or that you didn't; and will either levy a sanction against you or not. If you lose, you can appeal the ALJ's decision. If it loses, the FCC staff can also appeal it.[16] The pleading you file to effect such an appeal will be captioned a "Petition for Reconsideration" and will list the exceptions you take to the findings of the ALJ. If you do not appeal the Initial Decision within thirty days or if the FCC does not decide on its own to review it within fifty days, that decision becomes final.[17]

STEP 9: In most cases, Initial Decisions of Administrative Law Judges are subject to review by the Review Board, an internal Commission appellate body composed of three senior FCC employees. Your first appeal will likely be to the Review Board, which hears oral arguments on appeals and is directed by law to conform its decisions with all contest laws on the books, FCC contest policies and all past FCC contest decisions. The Review Board's determination after reviewing the ALJ's Initial Decision is known as a "Final Decision."[18]

STEP 10: Either you or the FCC staff can appeal the Review Board's decision to the five Commissioners of the FCC. The legal mechanism employed will again be a "Petition for Reconsideration" and must be filed within thirty days of the Review Board's Final Decision. The Commissioners may also directly order a decision of the Review Board before them for further review. Once finally before the FCC on appeal, the Commissioners may require oral argument, direct further legal briefs, and may closely scrutinize the full transcript of the initial hearing and examine all the evidence. The Commissioners can send the whole case back to the ALJ with orders to take further evidence or testimony, send the case back to the ALJ and direct that he or she issue a Supplemental Initial Decision modifying the Initial Decision, or issue its own decision on the record before it. The Commissioners' decision will contain their final determination of whether or not you violated the contest laws. It might also mete out a penalty.

Typically, these contest charges will be considered at the time you seek license renewal and the FCC will most often renew your license subject to some lesser sanction, such as sending a letter of reprimand, fining you or granting only a short-term renewal. Only in the most outrageous and rare cases will a license be revoked for contest misconduct. And with its decision, the agency will have spoken with force and finality.

STEP 11:   If you are found by the full FCC to have committed a contest infraction and the penalty imposed affected your license, you may challenge the decision. The route is to file an appeal with the United States Court of Appeals for the District of Columbia Circuit. That federal appellate court will either uphold the FCC's decision or overturn it; and its decision will be binding unless overruled by the Supreme Court.[19]

STEP 12:   The Circuit Court's decision can be appealed to the U.S. Supreme Court by either you or the FCC filing a petition for *certiorari*. If the Supreme Court grants *certiorari* and hears the case, its decision will settle the matter once and for all.[20]

If you go this far up the appellate ladder, you must resign yourself to the payment of very healthy attorneys' fees to vindicate your position. Some stations would rather put that kind of money in next week's Cash Call and try to attract some more listeners. (A factor which explains why so few broadcasters appeal even adverse decisions of the FCC.)

In the chapters which follow, the FCC procedural plumbing will come to life . . . virtually all contest cases decided by the Commission in the last fifty years will be discussed. Those chapters are organized on the basis of the penalty imposed— revocation of license, short-term renewal, fine and censure.

THE LIFE OF A CONTEST CASE AT THE FCC

STEP 1   FCC alerted to possible contest impropriety

STEP 2   FCC staff investigation

STEP 3   Subpoenaing of documents, interviewing of witnesses

STEP 4   The Commission reviews results of investigation; decides whether to prosecute

STEP 5   Issuance of a Notice of Designation for Hearing

STEP 6   Pre-hearing conference; consent agreement

STEP 7   The Hearing

STEP 8   Initial Decision of Administrative Law Judge

STEP 9   Review Board appeal

STEP 10   Appeal to the Commissioners of the FCC

STEP 11   Appeal to the U.S. Court of Appeals for the District of Columbia Circuit

STEP 12   Appeal to the U.S. Supreme Court

NOTES/5

1. *U.S. Government Printing Office, 48th Annual Report of the Federal Communications Commission,* Washington, D.C., 1982, pp. 105–122.

2. *National Broadcasting Co. v. United States,* 319 U.S. 190, 212 (1943).

3. *Ibid.,* 213.

4. Elizabeth B. Drew, "Is the FCC Dead?" *Atlantic,* July, 1967, p. 29.

5. Johnson and Dystel, "A Day in the Life: The Federal Communications Commission," 82 *Yale Law Review,* 1575, 1582 (1973).

6. *Ibid.,* 1584.

7. *Ibid.,* 1577.

8. Kenneth Cox, "Does the FCC Really Do Anything?" 11 *Journal of Broadcasting,* 97, 112 (1967).

9. 47 C.F.R. § 0.416 (1983).

10. 47 C.F.R. §§ 0.71, .111, .114 (1983).

11. 47 C.F.R. § 1.331 (1983).

12. 47 C.F.R. § 0.281 (1983).

13. 47 C.F.R. § 1.221 (1983).

14. 47 C.F.R. § 1.248 (1983).

15. 47 C.F.R. §§ 0.151, 1.243 (1983); 5 U.S.C. §§ 554, 556 (1982).

16. 47 C.F.R. §§ 1.267, 1.276 (1983); 5 U.S.C. § 557 (1982).

17. 47 C.F.R. § 1.276 (1983).

18. 47 C.F.R. §§ 0.5(b)(5), .361 (1983).

19. 47 U.S.C. § 402(b) (1982).

20. 47 U.S.C. § 402(j) (1982).

CHAPTER 6

Contests Which Resulted in Stations Losing Their Licenses

The Communications Act of 1934 specifically empowers the FCC to revoke the license of any station which violates contest integrity obligations.[1]

Contrary to the loud and emotional objections from Tucson's KIKX, there was solid precedent for the Commission's revocation of its license in the Crazy Man Craig disappearance. It had revoked other licenses for contest improprieties before. Indeed, the Tucson revocation was not only consistent with agency precedent, it was compelled by it and by the contest laws governing the case.

The FCC has occasionally imposed this sanction, often referred to as the "death penalty," in situations involving flagrant contest misconduct.

Miami, Florida

The license of WMJX-FM, Miami, was revoked in 1981 for improprieties involved in two separate contests.[2]

The 1975 "Find Greg Austin Contest," in which a popular disc jockey was falsely reported by WMJX to be wandering around the Miami area, dazed, his "mind boggled by the rough seas"[3] after a trip to the Bermuda Triangle, constituted one basis for the license revocation. The listener who found Austin would win the contest and a five hundred dollar grand prize. Contest promotions stated that WMJX was "really . . . concerned."[4] because he's "lost, no one has seen him."[5]

In truth, Austin was at the studio the day the contest was launched and WMJX announcers knew he had safely returned from his brief chartered boat excursion a few miles off shore.

The FCC also cited WMJX's 1975 "Easter Egg Hunt." In conjunction with that contest, WMJX had broadcast promotional announcements to the effect that the public could win a $1,000 prize inside one of the plastic eggs to be hidden. Ten days before the hunt, the station's program director learned the contest budget was depleted and that there'd be no big prize. Yet, he allowed the promos to continue.

The station vigorously resisted any FCC penalty and advanced five defenses. The Commission rejected each.

WMJX argued that the language in its promotional announcements was mere hyperbole and exaggeration. Retorted the FCC, "[T]he Commission has made clear that these very practices [exaggeration and overstatement] will not be tolerated in connection with contests and promotional announcements."[6]

The station protested that the FCC introduced no evidence of actual harm. The Commission noted its rule of evidence that "proof of actual injury to the public, . . . [is] not required to establish the wrong-doing."[7]

In response to WMJX's contention that the promotional announcements were ambiguous rather than patently deceptive, the FCC stated: "The licensee is responsible for broadcasting accurate statements as to the nature and value of contest prizes and will be held accountable for any announcement which tends to mislead the public."[8]

WMJX contended that no owners were personally involved in any wrongdoing and that the local station management and personnel had failed the owners. The FCC faulted the principals for not more closely supervising their employees to prevent such misconduct and imposed liability on the basis of *respondeat superior,* a legal doctrine making employers liable for the misdeeds of their employees.

The station also claimed that the First Amendment's free press guarantees protected such promotional announcements because they were commercial advertising and commercial speech. The FCC responded that fraudulent and misleading advertising does not enjoy constitutional protection.[9]

Dismissing all five of the station's arguments, the Commission ruled that there is "no excuse for frauds perpetrated upon the public;"[10] and insisted that every licensed broadcast station "as a public trustee, has an affirmative obligation to prevent the broadcast of false, misleading or deceptive contest announcements."[11] For gross and repeated violations of that obligation, the WMJX-FM license was revoked.

The WMJX decision is noteworthy for the Commission's concise responses to the defenses raised by the station. Too, the opinion's criticism of the station's general manager for never giving new employees "any instructions concerning Commission Rules and Regulations on contests and promotions . . ."[12] underscores that obligation which the agency obviously expects licensees to fulfill.

Indianapolis, Omaha and Vancouver

All five stations of the Star Stations of Indiana broadcast group lost their licenses in 1975 for a torrent of violations that included three instances of contest improprieties. The FCC revoked the licenses of WIFE and WIFE-FM in Indianapolis, KOIL and KOIL-FM in Omaha, and KISN in Vancouver, Wash. for misconduct in the broadcast of the "Eaton Water Filter Contest" on WIFE-FM, the WIFE "$1,000 Mystery Melody Contest," and the KOIL "Black Box Contest."[13]

The October 1964 "Eaton Water Filter Contest" offered listeners of WIFE-FM the opportunity to win three water filters, valued at $19.95 each, for correctly guessing "how many gallons of water could pass through"[14] one of the Eaton filters during a week's time.

However, no entries were received. The station concealed that fact from Eaton and designated as the three contest winners a WIFE-FM secretary, a receptionist and the wife of a salesman at the station. Although a conflict in testimony prevented the commission from concluding the station owner—Donald Burden—was personally involved in the scenario,[15] it found "WIFE's actions with respect thereto constituted a fraud."[16]

Subsequently investigating the two other contest complaints, the FCC decided "Burden's continued derelictions in conducting promotional contests . . . are a serious reflection on his ability and willingness to protect the public from these irregularities."[17] Including other instances in which Burden had compromised the integrity of his stations, particularly news slanting and misrepresentations to the FCC, the agency concluded "Star's principals and employees have demonstrated a pattern of conduct which we find reprehensible."[18] and revoked all five licenses.

The Commission's decision was affirmed by the U.S. Court of Appeals, and the U.S. Supreme Court denied *certiorari*.[19]

Unquestionably, the wholesale revocation of five valuable broadcast licenses constitutes a severe and sweeping penalty; and reflects the seriousness with which the FCC views contest integrity.

Milton, Florida

Milton station WSRA conducted two contests in 1965 for which its license was revoked.[20] The station's Christmas home lighting and decorating contest offered cash prizes to listeners. Whoever best incorporated "WSRA" into his or her holiday decorations would be declared the winner. Yet, the money was never awarded. When a listener asked who had won, the president of the station furnished a fictitious name, which was broadcast on the air.

WSRA's "Thanksgiving Turkey Shoot" invited listeners to guess how many shots it would take to fell that hour's fictional turkey. The disc jockey had access to several cartridge tapes, each labeled with the number of gunshots recorded on it. Once the listener made a guess, the disc jockey would often select a tape, not at random, but knowing how many shots were on it. If he wanted the caller to win, he would select the appropriate tape. Otherwise, a losing tape was played.

The FCC revoked the license, determining that WSRA's misconduct in each contest constituted the unlawful prearranging of the outcomes of the contests, in direct violation of Section 509(a)(3) of the Communications Act.[21]

St. Louis, Missouri

St. Louis radio station KWK broadcast a "Treasure Hunt Contest" in 1960 which ran for nearly four weeks. During that time, promotional announcements alerted listeners that the treasure was hidden in a public place somewhere in the St. Louis area. Clues were broadcast as to its precise location.[22]

An FCC investigation subsequently revealed, however, that KWK's general manager had waited until the final day of the contest to hide the treasure. For four weeks, contestants had been searching St. Louis for something that hadn't even left the station.

The FCC characterized the station's conduct as fraudulent and deceitful, reasoning that "[t]he perpetration of deliberate frauds upon the public is patently and flagrantly contrary to the public interest and cannot be countenanced. . . ."[23]

The station's owners argued in their defense that they had neither knowledge of nor involvement in the misdeeds of their employees. Rejecting that contention, the Commission faulted the station's principals for not taking the precautions or exercising the supervision of their employees necessary to prevent contest misconduct:

> [I]n conducting treasure hunts, a high degree of responsibility devolved upon KWK to effectuate reasonable safeguards which would reasonably assure that no frauds or deceptions would be perpetrated on the public.[24]

For conducting fraudulent contests, KWK's license was revoked. The statutory basis for the penalty was Section 312(a)(2) and (3) of the Communications Act, which allows revocations for conduct which would have justified the FCC to refuse to originally license the station. The Commission based the severity of its sanction on "the philosophy of holding licensees to an exemplary standard of conduct in contest-type programs and the grave concern of Congress with frauds upon the public. . . ."[25]

The U.S. Court of Appeals affirmed the FCC, holding "the record clearly supports the findings and conclusions of the Commission."[26] The U.S. Supreme Court denied *certiorari*.[27]

The Commission's KWK decision is illuminating in a number of respects. First, certainly for its articulation of the "exemplary standard of conduct in contest-type programs" to which it will hold its licensees. Second, the reaffirmation of the duty of station owners to adopt contest safeguards and exercise close supervision of their employees. Third, the conclusion that contest frauds are contrary to the public interest has significant prospective force since violations of the public interest obligation constitute a separate statutory basis for license revocation or other sanction.[28] And fourth, this decision is noteworthy for utilizing Section 312(a)(2) and (3) for license revocation.

Pasadena, California

Pasadena radio station KRLA was stripped of its license for broadcasting a fraudulent contest in 1959.[29] The "Find Perry Allen Contest" was designed to focus listener attention on the station's newest disc jockey. As listeners in the Los Angeles-Pasadena area had yet to meet him, KRLA devised this contest and broadcast daily clues as to Allen's appearance.

Listeners were told he could be found in Los Angeles restaurants or ball parks. One clue that aired described him as wearing a grey suit and a bow tie. Listeners were invited to confront people answering the descriptions and ask if they were Perry Allen, the newest KRLA personality.

While KRLA broadcast these clues and convinced untold numbers of listeners to go to restaurants in search of bow ties, Allen was still working in Buffalo, N.Y., at his old job, waiting to move to California. From Buffalo, Allen taped twelve clues and promotional announcements per day for a ten days' supply to be aired in Pasadena.

On the second day of the contest, Allen was located in Buffalo by a rival radio station.

The FCC determined that the contest was "fraudulent in the sense that various clues which were broadcast . . . were deceptive, and knowingly so."[30] Aggravating the station's case was other misconduct which was unearthed during the FCC investigation, including a finding that official station program logs had been altered to reflect programs not actually broadcast. Deeming such attempts to mislead the FCC as precluding license renewal, the Commission characterized station management as neglectful and its course of conduct as a "continued pattern of deception,"[31] and revoked the license. The U.S. Court of appeals affirmed and the U.S. Supreme Court declined review.[32]

The legal precedent of this decision as it applies to contests is doubtful because of the accumulation of other, even more egregious misconduct by this station.[33] Yet, the obvious contest fraud at KRLA certainly constituted one of the bases for the license revocation.

While the FCC has employed this ultimate sanction infrequently and "pulled the plug" only on those stations whose contest misconduct was uniquely outrageous, its arsenal of lesser sanctions has often been tapped. The four chapters which follow focus on those cases.

NOTES/6

1. 47 U.S.C. §§ 312(a)(4), 312(a)(6) (1982).

2. WMJX, Inc., 85 F.C.C.2d 251 (1981).

3. *Ibid.*, 257.

4. *Ibid.*

5. *Ibid.*

6. *Ibid.*, 273.

7. *Ibid.*, 270.

8. *Ibid.*, 272.

9. *Ibid.*, 277, at note 120.

10. *Ibid.*, 274.

11. *Ibid.*, 269.

12. *Ibid.*

13. *Star Stations of Indiana, Inc.*, 51 F.C.C.2d 95 (1975), *aff'd sub. nom. Star Stations, Inc., v. F.C.C.*, 527 F.2d 853 (D.C. Cir. 1975), *cert. denied* 425 U.S. 992 (1976).

14. *Star Stations of Indiana, Inc.*, 19 F.C.C.2d 1012, 1013 (1967).

15. At one point, Station Manager Ronald Mercer claimed full responsibility for the conduct of the contest. At the FCC hearing, however, he testified that Burden had told him to "go get some winners" when advised that no one had in fact entered. Mercer contended Burden then directed the fraud and concealment. Burden denied any such knowledge or act. *Star Stations of Indiana, Inc.*, 19 F.C.C.2d 991, 1006 (1969).

16. *Star Stations of Indiana, Inc.*, 19 F.C.C.2d 991, 992 (1969).

17. *Star Stations of Indiana, Inc.*, *supra* note 13 at 108.

18. *Ibid.,* 107.

19. *Aff'd sub nom., Star Stations Inc. v. F.C.C.,* 527 F.2d 853 (D.C. Cir. 1975), *cert. denied,* 425 U.S. 992 (1976).

20. *Santa Rosa Broadcasting Co., Inc.,* 9 F.C.C.2d 644 (1967).

21. It is noted that counsel for this licensee did not proceed at the FCC's preliminary conference due to the bankruptcy of Santa Rosa's majority stockholder. The Administrative Law Judge then held Santa Rosa in default, conducted no hearing, and directly certified the case to the Commission for its decision. Whether this default and the failure of Santa Rosa to mount a full defense vitiates the impact or precedential value of the decision should be considered. Due to the obvious nature of the § 509 violations, however, and given the Commission precedent on point, it is highly doubtful the FCC would have declined to impose a severe penalty. The only truly debatable issue is whether a vigorous defense would have saved the license from revocation and won a short-term renewal or fine instead.

22. *KWK Radio, Inc.,* 34 FCC 1039 (1963).

23. *Ibid.,* 1041.

24. *Ibid.,* 1042.

25. *KWK Radio, Inc.,* 35 FCC 561, 564 (1963).

26. *KWK Radio, Inc. v. Federal Communications Commission,* 337 F.2d 540, 541 (D.C. Cir. (1964).

27. *Cert. denied,* 380 U.S. 910 (1965).

28. No radio or television station broadcast license can be granted or renewed unless its holder is broadcasting in the public interest. 47 U.S.C. §§ 301, 307, 308, 309 (1982).

29. *Eleven Ten Broadcasting Corp.,* 32 FCC 706 (1962), *recon. denied,* 33 FCC 92 (1962).

30. *Ibid.,* 707.

31. *Ibid.,* 712.

32. *Aff'd sub nom, Immaculate Conception Church of Los Angeles et al. v. F.C.C.*, 320 F.2d 795 (D.C. Cir. 1963), *cert. denied*, 375 U.S. 904 (1964).

33. As the FCC noted in a later decision distinguishing the Eleven Ten case: ''it was not the contest violation alone, but the violation plus the licensee's efforts to mislead the Commission, which resulted in . . . the decision to deny renewal.'' *Oil Shale Broadcasting Company*, 68 F.C.C.2d 517, 528 (1978).

CHAPTER 7

Contests for Which Stations Were Granted Only Short-Term License Renewals

The FCC is authorized by statute[1] to impose the penalty of a short-term renewal. Under this option, the Commission typically renews a license for a one-year term only, rather than for the full statutory license term of five or seven years.

During that short-term renewal period, the license is considered on probation and its activities—particularly concerning the violations that led to the short-term punishment—are monitored by the FCC. If, at the end of that probationary period, the station's operation is evaluated as satisfactory and in compliance with the rules, the license may be renewed, upon proper additional application, for a full term.

Broadcasters regard short-term renewals as serious and costly retributions. The enormous legal fees and station management time needed to re-apply within a year for a new license are especially burdensome. Too, the cloud that hangs over the station during the year's probation is acutely embarrassing for a business operation chartered to serve the public interest and which inherently maintains high community visibility. Word of such an FCC penalty is public record and heralded in a full published FCC decision released in Washington. And the local newspaper rivals of stations so punished are often quick to prominently report such news in the hometown.

Over the years, the FCC has liberally employed the short-term renewal to redress violations of its contest rules.

Panama City, Florida

The 1975 "Play WGNE Contest" in Panama City exploded into a station nightmare early in the contest when two listeners won the grand prize in one single day. Action was immediately taken by the station's program director to eliminate any repetition of that assault on the cash register.[2]

Simple enough in its conception, the contest involved listeners calling the station and guessing whether the letters W, G, N or E would come up next, roulette-style, on a cartridge tape held by the disc jockey. The program director rigged the contest by merely labeling the pre-recorded cartridges by letter.

The Commission majority rejected the decision of the Administrative Law Judge that license revocation was merited by this obvious violation of the provisions of Section 509 of the Communications Act prohibiting prearrangement or fixing of contest outcome. It did hold that "the misconduct is too serious to be countenanced by the Commission,"[3] and renewed the license only on a short-term basis.

Rifle, Colorado

The November 1973 contest of KWSR, where listeners could win holiday turkeys, consisted of an announcer making a phone call each hour. A recorded sequence of ten animal sounds was then played. If the distinctive warbling of a turkey was among the ten, the listener would win a frozen turkey.[4]

Yet, some winners were selected in advance, including one person who advertised heavily on the station. And contrary to broadcast contest rules, other entry post cards were not chosen at random but were pre-selected on the basis of hometown to ensure a wide geographic representation. To effect the fraud, the announcers would listen to the tape cartridges in advance, select the animals they wished to air, and decide whether a turkey would be among the ten on a particular tape.

While acknowledging that the principal of the corporate owner of the station was not "knowingly involved in the contest violations,"[5] the Commission held him "responsible for exercising proper control and supervision over his employees in order to ensure compliance"[6] with the contest laws.

On that basis, the owner was held accountable for the violations of Section 509 and the FCC imposed a short-term license renewal.

Center Court

Despite the frequent promotion by CBS television that its "Heavyweight Championship of Tennis" series of four matches between Jimmy Connors and various challengers between 1975 and 1977 was "winner-take-all," an investigation revealed that each loser was guaranteed at least $150,000 and that CBS knew it.[7]

Characterizing the CBS promos as "false or misleading statements to the public,''[8] the FCC faulted the network for "repeated instances of public deception."[9]

The uniqueness of the fact situation presented here was that the tennis contest itself was not rigged and therefore there was no violation of Section 509. The significance of the case is that the FCC fashioned an alternative means to impose a sanction against CBS anyway. The Commission reasoned that the broadcast of misleading contest promos constituted public deception and that such deception violated two obligations owed the public and the FCC by all broadcast stations: the obligation to operate in the public interest and the duty to exercise supervision over operations sufficient to ensure that no false and misleading material is ever broadcast as true over the air. For violating those obligations, the Commission ordered a short-term renewal for the CBS network owned-and-operated television station in Los Angeles, KNXT.[10]

It should be noted that during the pendency of this case, CBS adopted new "internal procedures designed to prevent recurrence of the deceptive practices"[11] which included requiring all network sports employees to certify in writing that they had read the new guidelines and understood them. And, before the FCC vote, President Gene F. Jankowski of the CBS Broadcast stations appeared on a special seven-minute network report to the people and admitted that the network's references to winner-take-all had been "wrong and misleading"[12] and had deceived the public.

The FCC applauded those corrective measures as effective in preventing future deception and opted for this second-level sanction rather than entertain license revocation partly as a result of the new procedures and public admission of responsibility for the misleading statements.

In a dissent to the majority's decision, Commissioner James H. Quello argued that "such exaggerated promotion [should not be placed] on the egregious level of a deliberately rigged performance intended to deceive the public."[13] Rejecting the alternative basis for imposition of the penalty, he insisted that "[t]he contest itself was not rigged"[14] and therefore the broadcaster should not be subject to such a severe sanction.

Milford, Connecticut

In conjunction with the 1976 Ali-Norton championship prize fight, Milford station WFIF conducted an "Ali-Norton Knock Out Contest."

To win, listeners were to correctly guess whether or not they could knock out Ali in a simulated one-minute bout which had been previously recorded on cartridge tape. At the conclusion of the taped bout aired by the disc jockey while the listener remained on the line, the ring referee would announce the winner —Ali or the challenger.

It was WFIF, however, that was knocked out when the FCC discovered that each disc jockey had two distinctly marked tapes —a "win" tape and a "lose" tape. The station even posted a schedule in the studio as to which tape was to be played at what times. For instance:

Tuesday	1 p.m.—lose
	3 p.m.—lose
	5 p.m.—lose
Wednesday	8 a.m.—winner.[15]

Characterizing such blatant prearrangement of the outcome as intolerable deception, the Commission directed a short-term license renewal.

Braddock Heights, Maryland

Braddock Heights station WZYQ-FM broadcast a "14 ZYQ Will Make Me Rich Contest" in 1976. Area residents who answered their home telephones "14 ZYQ Will Make Me Rich" rather than "Hello" would, if randomly called by the station, win "a prize package of dollars"[16] which would make them, as announced, rich.

Two winners, however, received only thirty dollars in cash and the remaining several hundreds of dollars in non-cash prizes; and they complained to the FCC that they had been duped by the promise of a large cash award.

The FCC decided that "the phrases 'a prize package of dollars' and 'cash prize jackpot' would lead a reasonable person to conclude that an all-cash prize was being offered to the winner"[17] and determined therefore that the station had misled and deceived its listeners.

The Commission imposed a short-term renewal on WZYQ for violating its 1974 Public Notice which prohibited the broadcasting of false or misleading prize information.

Zanesville, Ohio

In announcing a quarter-million dollar contest in 1975 to its Zanesville listeners, station WOMP broadcast promotional announcements which began: "You [echo] . . . could win thousands of dollars in the Pot of Gold Funtest. . . ."[18]

To enter, listeners were told to mail postcards with their names and addresses to WOMP. The winner would be drawn on May 12, 1975.

The station's general manager stated on the air that $250,000 could be won. In truth, on the day of the drawing, he revealed that the prizes were fifty Ohio State Lottery tickets.

The FCC charged that the promos conveyed "the unmistakable impression that the only requirement for winning money was selection of the listener's postcard"[19] and not the further and very slim chance he or she would win in the state lottery out of tens of thousands of other lottery ticket holders to ever collect any money.

WOMP insisted in its defense that if the listeners had paid close attention to what was said on the air about the contest, "it was patently clear that the station would only . . . make them eligible to win in the Ohio State Lottery."[20]

Yet, an FCC field investigation disclosed that even WOMP's own announcers "believed that cash prizes were to be awarded,"[21] rather than lottery tickets and did not learn otherwise until the day of the drawing.

The Commission ruled that by airing misleading contest promos, WOMP had violated its 1974 Public Notice which expressly prohibited such conduct. For that violation, the station was given a short-term renewal.

Lubbock, Texas

Upon the admission by Lubbock station KLFB that one of its vice presidents, Marcos Garcia, had purposely removed the names of Anglo entrants which had been submitted as contestants in a 1973 station promotion, the FCC determined "such conduct represents a serious breach of licensee responsibility."[22]

Particularly, the Commission held such activity to prearrange the contest's outcome violated its policy statements announced in previous cases that "contests should be conducted fairly and substantially as represented to the public."[23] For that breach, the station received a short-term renewal.

Honolulu, Hawaii

The reach of the 1974 Public Notice was tested when Honolulu station KPOI vigorously resisted FCC sanctions for what the government argued were misleading contest bumper stickers and pamphlets.

At issue was a 1974 "$100,000 Cash Fall Contest" in which the station awarded only $34,000 in prizes. The FCC insisted that the language used in promoting the contest conveyed the impression to listeners that fully $100,000 would be awarded.

KPOI maintained in its defense that the "$100,000 Cash

Fall'' ads were never aired on the station but were published in 40,000 pamphlets and bumper stickers distributed in the city. Because of that, KPOI reasoned, whatever was stated or implied to the listeners was beyond the FCC's jurisdiction since the Commission's reach ended at the station's exit door and did not extend to the parking lots of Honolulu.

But the Commission determined that KPOI's promotion of its ''$100,000 Cash Fall'' violated the 1974 Public Notice provisions regarding not only the failure to award all prizes as announced, but also outlawing misleading contest information. The agency correctly noted that the 1974 Public Notice prohibits ''disseminating false or misleading''[24] contest prize information.

The Commission reasoned that such language, notably the use of ''disseminating'' rather than ''broadcasting,'' clearly encompassed printed brochures and stickers and that, to be actionable, misleading contest promotions do not need to be broadcast on the air.

Concluding that the promotion employed was misleading, the FCC imposed a short-term renewal on KPOI.

Denver, Colorado

Denver radio station KTLK's ''Miss Miniskirt Contest,'' which was designed ''to rally support for the miniskirt''[25] in 1970 when fashion designers were predicting its extinction, caused such tumult in downtown Denver that fifteen police officers were called to restore order.

Contestants, wearing their favorite mini's, paraded on the marquee of a downtown theatre vying for the title ''Miss Miniskirt.''

The contest, which began at noon and continued forty-five minutes, attracted nearly 1,000 onlookers. As the crowd grew, pedestrians wandered into lanes of traffic to get a better view of the spectacle above. Traffic in the block in front of the theatre slowed and jammed three blocks back. Police officers at the scene were forced to request assistance to control the traffic congestion.

The FCC concluded that KTLK's contest violated its 1966 Public Notice which expressly prohibited contests which caused "traffic congestion or other public disorder requiring diversion of police from other duties;"[26] and directed a short-term renewal.

At the same time, the Commission investigated internal station operations and discovered that the broadcaster had "failed to give adequate instructions to its employees as to the manner in which [contests] . . . should be conducted. . . ."[27] The FCC emphasized that such responsibility to instruct employees regarding the proper, lawful conduct of contests must be met by station owners; and this point of emphasis in the decision is significant for the clear obligation it imposes on broadcasters to plainly explain the law regarding contests to all employees.

Louisa, Kentucky

Station WVKY broadcast a "Jackpot Bowling Contest" in 1973. When so many contestants started winning that the station's weekly contest budget was exceeded in just two days, the general manager took steps to rig the contest from there on out.

The contest operated in this way. Listeners wishing to enter sent cards with their names and phone numbers. Cards would be randomly drawn and a disc jockey would call the person on the air. The contestant would win the cash in the jackpot if he or she correctly predicted which of three bowling ball rolls the cartridge tape about to be played contained—a strike, a gutter ball or pins left standing.

Once the contestant guessed, WVKY's disc jockey would punch up whatever tape was next and the listening audience would hear the sound of a ball rolling down an alley and either connecting with the pins or not.

After the decision to rig the contest was made, the disc jockeys would juggle the cartridge tapes so that whatever ball the contestant predicted would not be heard. The deejay would simply play one of the other two marked tapes and the contestant would lose.

Given the evidence that the general manager "admitted that he instructed the announcers to predetermine the result of the contest in order to control the number of winners,"[28] the FCC found that WVKY had violated Section 509 of the Communications Act and issued a short-term renewal.

Wheeling, West Virginia

A 1972 amateur golf tournament, the "XL-95 Golf Classic," was organized and heavily promoted by station WXLW in Wheeling.

Daily broadcast announcements stated that local golfers could win "over $25,000 in prizes."[29] Yet, in truth, $10,000 was reserved for a companion celebrity tournament and another $9,000 could be won by the amateurs only for holes-in-one.

The FCC charged that WXLW had misled the public by not explaining the difficult conditions for winning such a large percentage of the prize money, and that failing to mention the hole-in-one requirement in its promotional announcements was a "substantial omission"[30] for which the station should incur liability.

The station insisted it had no intent to deceive or mislead the public and that the use of the offending language had been unwitting and purely unintentional.

The Commission decided that such lack of intent is no defense in contest cases. It noted, instead, that its 1961 Public Notice required that the FCC satisfy itself on only one issue before inflicting a contest penalty: whether the station expended reasonable efforts "to assure that deceptive advertising is not broadcast. . . ."[31]

Concluding that WXLW had not taken such steps, the FCC ordered a short-term renewal for the failure to take all reasonable measures to eliminate the misleading golf promos.

A quite significant aspect of this decision is its embrace of a strict liability or quasi-strict liability rule. Strict liability is a legal term that means liability without fault. Under such rationale, intent to commit a crime or violation is not necessary for conviction—the only requirement is that the violation occur, even accidentally.

Obviously, the broadcaster's lack of intent to mislead or deceive will not save him as long as the FCC continues to employ this strict liability standard. The Commission appears to follow this logic: if a station broadcasts false or misleading contest promos, liability will attach unless it can be shown that the station took all reasonable steps to eliminate such deceptive promos. A rather curious question remains, however: in what circumstances could a station which took such steps and eliminated such deceptive matter ever air a single deceptive promo, anyway?

The only evidence a broadcaster could successfully offer in defense would appear to be a showing that all conceivable steps had in fact been taken (owners instructing the station employees on the legal aspects of broadcast contests, owners closely controlling and supervising their employees' subsequent contest conduct, and whatever other steps were taken) and yet false, deceptive or misleading matter was somehow broadcast in spite of the best efforts of station ownership and management.

Richmond, Virginia

A 1971 contest conducted by WENZ precipitated an unusual Commission response which clearly broke new ground.

The idea of the contest was that listeners were instructed to set their radio dials to WENZ, then remove the tuning knob and send it to the station, tagged with the owner's name and address. A drawing was to be held to select the winning knob and that lucky contestant would receive a stereo radio console.

Although the last day for entries was June 7, 1970, the station did not award the prize until more than a year later—August 4, 1971. But the facts presented a dilemma for Commission action.

Had the station's promotional announcements represented that the drawing would be held on, for instance, June 7, 1970, and the winner announced and the prize awarded at that time, the FCC could easily have determined such promo was false and misleading and thus violated the 1961 Public Notice, and on that basis imposed sanctions.

Here, however, the station's announcements did not commit it to a specific prize delivery date. To impose liability, the Commission fashioned an alternative basis—that of "reasonableness" in the conduct of a contest.

It held that "prizes should be awarded within a reasonable period of time after the end of the contest"[32] and that the one year delay "in this case was unreasonable."[33] For violating this standard of contest conduct, WENZ was given a short-term renewal.

It should be noted that two years after this decision, the FCC issued a Public Notice specifically warning licensees that contest prizes must be awarded "within a reasonable time."[34]

The importance of the WENZ decision is that the Commission boldly extended its reach into contest conduct which was not at the time specifically prohibited by rule or public notice. Yet in the Commission's view, it was "unreasonable" conduct. This alternative basis for liability opens up virtually any aspect of a broadcaster's contest conduct to FCC scrutiny.

Kahului, Hawaii

Kahului station KNUI broadcast a poster contest in 1971 which challenged its listeners' visual keenness.

Various business sponsors around the city would display printed posters of a man fully dressed. All were exactly alike, except two which showed the man with one pen in his pocket rather than two.

To win, a listener was required to identify by mail the merchants displaying the two variant posters. The earliest post-marked correct answer was to receive a color TV set.

The contest ran from August 2 until September 14, 1971; and announcements were broadcast throughout that period explaining how to win.

But, despite the August 2 starting date for the frequent promotional announcements, the first winning poster was not placed in a business's window until August 13. The second winning poster was not distributed until August 31—a full four weeks after the start of the six-week contest.

The FCC charged KNUI "manipulated the duration of the contest and broadcast false and misleading advertising pertaining to the contest."[35] It decided that the station's deliberate poster distribution delay was precisely the type of "artifice or scheme prohibited by [Section 509 of] the Act"[36] and that it was patent prearrangement of the contest outcome. The Commission imposed a short-term renewal for the violation.

Carlsbad, New Mexico

The 1971 "Treasure Chest Contest" of station KCCC afforded contestants the opportunity to stop by the studio and select an envelope from among hundreds piled in a two-foot by two-foot treasure chest. A new drawing was held each month.

KCCC publicity announced that one of the envelopes contained a card entitling the contestant to $1,900 in prizes. Yet, when the FCC inventoried the chest after the October contest, it found no grand prize envelope.

The station explained that its studio had been broken into and its files ransacked. It was possible, KCCC argued, that the intruder(s) also rifled the treasure chest and took several of the prize envelopes.

The Commission resolved the case without a direct finding of fact concerning the burglary scenario. It emphasized that it imposes on licensees the duty to ''adequately supervise and control the contests to assure that they are conducted fairly and are substantially as represented in announcements to the public.''[37]

KCCC had breached that duty, the agency held, because it failed to inventory the contents of the chest before the October contest to satisfy itself that no intruder had tampered with it and that the grand prize could still be won. Once again, a short-term renewal was imposed for the violation.

The affirmative obligation the FCC articulates in the KCCC case apparently requires continuous vigilance and activity by the broadcaster in terms of contest security and integrity throughout the contest.

Richmond, Virginia

One of the most interesting contest fact situations involves the ''Snow Fall Contest'' conducted by Richmond's WEKY in 1969. The station advertised that the listener correctly guessing the date of the first snowfall of the year would win ''the keys to a new Impala.''[38]

And, the station in fact awarded one Mr. Wall, the contest winner, said keys—but no car to go with them. Shocked, Wall demanded his wheels. Adamant, WEKY insisted it never intended to give away a prize as extravagant as a new car and that its promotional announcements promised no more than just the keys.

Wall then enlisted the aid of the FCC. The station attempted to pacify Mr. Wall by sending him a little toy car with a twenty dollar bill rolled up inside. Wall was not moved by the gesture.

When the FCC attempted to encourage the station to honor its representations and reach a compromise with Wall, WEKY resisted and argued it would be "an unfair penalty to require him to provide a car." [39]

After its best efforts at negotiation failed, the FCC resorted to its arsenal of sanctions and chose a short-term renewal as an appropriate penalty. The Commission reasoned that the plain language of the promos "would lead a reasonable person to the conclusion that a new 1970 Chevrolet Impala automobile was being offered to the winner." [40]

Characterizing those announcements as false, deceptive and misleading, the FCC determined that such statements contravened its 1961 Public Notice requiring honesty, fairness and forthrightness.

Too, this case should be noted for the Commission's use of the "reasonable man" standard in interpreting whether the language and advertising at issue is deceptive or misleading. That is, whether the representations made by the station would be misleading to a person of average intellect in the community who possessed common sense and experience as a consumer.

Springfield, Illinois

The 1967 "Lucky Bucks Contest" of WCVS involved station personnel distributing numerous one dollar bills throughout the Springfield area. This was accomplished without fanfare, with the bills being used, for instance, to purchase ordinary household items at stores.

The station maintained a master list of the serial numbers of all bills it circulated. Five times each day, a disc jockey would read the *last digit* of one of the eight-digit serial numbers over the air. If the listener in Springfield (1967 population approximately 85,000) with the winning serial number immediately called the station and was one of the first five callers, he or she would win the contest and from $1,000 to $100,000. Of course, the clairvoyance required for anyone to deduce from the announcement of one digit of an 8-digit serial number that he or she in fact held the bill in question—the winning bill—is phenomenal. Yet the WCVS promotional advertisements stated that $100,000 was being "offered"[41] and was being "given away."[42]

The FCC contended the ads were misleading because "the chances of $100,000 (or any amount coming close to that sum) being given away were virtually nonexistent."[43] Holding that such advertising contravened its 1961 Public Notice, the agency imposed a short-term renewal.

This decision also addressed the question of how the Commission would determine whether or not an ad is misleading:

> If the net impression of the announcements has a tendency
> to mislead the public, that is enough.[44]

With WCVS, the Commission conceded the ads were "not technically false"[45] but concluded their net impact was to mislead the public into believing there were decent chances of winning. Such deception, even though fashioned through facially true promotional announcements, was held actionable.

Charleston, West Virginia

A similar contest was broadcast by Charleston station WCHS-AM. Its 1965 "Lucky Bucks Contest" also involved the distribution of dollar bills and the reading of winning serial numbers. Again, the FCC's consternation was ignited by evidence that it was "virtually impossible to win more than a small predetermined fraction of the prize total offered each week."[46]

The WCHS contest promotionals had stated that $6,000 in cash could be won each week. Yet, the average amount actually awarded weekly was thirty dollars.

Based on the stark disparity between money offered and actually won, the FCC decided the advertising regarding the $6,000 was false, misleading and deceptive in violation of the 1961 Public Notice. A short-term renewal was ordered.[47]

Evolving from WCHS is another factor the FCC considers as evidence of whether or not an ad is misleading—the disparity quotient. A mathematically significant variance between prize money offered and that eventually awarded indicates the offer broadcast was misleading.

NOTES/7

1.   47 U.S.C. § 307(c) (1982).

2.   *Janus Broadcasting Company,* 78 FCC 2d 788 (1980).

3.   *Ibid.,* 793.

4.   *Oil Shale Broadcasting Company,* 68 FCC 2d 517 (1978).

5.   *Ibid.,* 518.

6.   *Ibid.,* 523.

7.   *CBS, Inc., Tennis Match,* 67 FCC 2d 969 (1978).

8.   *Ibid.,* 970.

9.   *Ibid.,* 972.

10. Letter from Howard F. Jaeckel, Assistant General Attorney, Law Department, CBS, Inc., July 25, 1983.

11. *CBS, Inc.,* 69 FCC 2d 1082, 1085 (1978).

12. *Ibid.*

13. *Ibid.,* 1095.

14. *Ibid.*

15. *Colonial Broadcasting Co.,* 44 Rad. Reg. 2d 1191, 1192 (1978).

16. *Musical Heights, Inc.,* 40 Rad. Reg. 2d 1016, 1017 (1977).

17. *Ibid.*

18. *T/R, Inc.,* 38 Rad. Reg. 2d 1310, 1311 (1976).

19. *Ibid.*

20. *Ibid.*

21. *Ibid.,* 1312.

22. *LaFiesta Broadcasting, Inc.,* 59 FCC 2d 1175, 1178 (1976).

23. *Ibid.*

24. *Communico Oceanic Corp.*, 55 FCC 2d 733, 736 (1975).

25. *Action Radio, Inc.*, 51 FCC 2d 811, 820 (1973) [decision of Administrative Law Judge].

26. *Action Radio, Inc.*, 51 FCC 2d 803, 804 (1975).

27. *Ibid.*, 808.

28. *Lawrence County Broadcasting Corp.*, 45 FCC 2d 881, 882 (1974).

29. *Greater Indianapolis Broadcasting Company, Inc.*, 44 FCC 2d 599, 600 (1973).

30. *Ibid.*, 600.

31. *Ibid.*

32. *Baron Radio Inc.*, 25 Rad. Reg. 2d 1125 (1972).

33. *Ibid.*

34. *Public Notice Concerning Failure of Broadcast Licensees to Conduct Contests Fairly*, 45 FCC 2d 1056, 1057 (1974).

35. *Qualitron Aero, Inc.*, 25 Rad. Reg. 2d 679, 682 (1972).

36. *Ibid.*

37. *KOLOB Broadcasting Co.*, 36 FCC 2d 586, 587 (1972).

38. *Henkin, Inc.*, 29 FCC 2d 40, 42 (1971).

39. *Ibid.*

40. *Ibid.*, 40.

41. *Eastern Broadcasting Corp.*, 14 FCC 2d 228 (1968).

42. *Ibid.*

43. *Ibid.*

44. *Ibid.*, 229.

45. *Ibid.*

46. *WCHS-AM-TV Corp.*, 4 FCC 2d 376 (1966).

47. *WCHS-AM-TV Corp.*, 8 FCC 2d 608 (1967)

CHAPTER 8

Contests for Which Stations Were Fined

The Communications Act empowers the FCC to fine any station which violates the contest laws.[1] Technically, these fines are called forfeitures. Regardless of terminology, when enacted they are direct hits on a station's cash register; and for that reason alone are serious threats.

While the Commission is responsible for determining the exact amount of the fine, its discretion in setting the penalty is restrained by law and the amount of the fine is limited by the Act. For example, the fine must not exceed $2,000 a day, and although each day the offense continues (that is, each day a fraudulent contest continues on the air) constitutes a separate offense, the total forfeiture may not exceed $20,000.[2]

The Commission must also consider certain factors when setting the fines, including the gravity of the offense, any history of prior offenses, and a station's financial status and ability to pay.[3]

Armed with this forfeiture authority, the Commission has imposed fines against broadcast stations on six separate occasions for violating contest rules.

Washington, D.C.

In 1978, the FCC assessed a $6,000 forfeiture against WOOK-FM for operating a "Black Book Contest." To enter, listeners would submit their own names and the names of three friends. The station would then randomly telephone the friends and award prizes to those listening to WOOK.

However, a Commission investigation revealed the station's promotion and conduct of the contest violated its regulations in two ways.

First, in promoting the contest on the air, WOOK never indicated what prizes could be won. Instead, individual winners were told only after the calls were made. The FCC determined such illusiveness violated the requirement of Code Section 73.1216 that the station fully disclose all material terms of the contest.

Secondly, the promos for the contest stated that any Black Book winners would automatically become eligible "to win in any [WOOK-FM] . . . contest for the entire year of 1978."[4] But when WOOK refused to declare several Black Book winners qualified to compete in its subsequent lucrative "Thousand Dollar Dial Contest," the FCC charged its rule prohibiting false, misleading or deceptive contest promos had been violated.

In fining the station, the Commission explained for the record why it took contest improprieties so much more seriously than violations of its other technical and engineering rules:

> [W]e believe forfeitures for violations of the contest rule
> should be for greater amounts than those imposed for viola-
> tions for matters not so directly affecting the public.[5]

Thus, the WOOK decision is also noteworthy for its acknowl-
edgment that because so many listeners and viewers participate
in contests, prosecution for contest improprieties should be a
priority of this federal agency charged with the duty of protecting the public's interests. This certainly contributes to an understanding of why the FCC is quick to move against contest misconduct and offers insight into the mindset of the agency.

Portsmouth, Virginia

In 1977, Portsmouth station WHNE sponsored a "Mr. Treasure Contest" which gave listeners the chance to win $2,000 for
finding a special medicine bottle the station had hidden in Virginia Beach. To promote the contest and help listeners locate the
bottle, the station broadcast several clues.

One such clue stated that the bottle was "not hidden . . . on
any private property."[6] In truth, however, the bottle was partially buried in a privately-owned vacant lot across from a shopping
mall.

Characterizing that clue as patently false and misleading, the
FCC spoke plainly of the interest of the public which under-
pinned its decision: "[T]here were individuals who were misled
by these announcements."[7] WHNE was fined $5,000 for violat-
ing the precise prohibition against misleading promos contained
in Section 73.1216 of the Rules.

Responding to the station's defense that it never intended to
mislead the public, the Commission noted the "strict liability"
nature of these violations:

> Such a finding [of intent] is not necessary to impose a
> forfeiture for violation of Section 73.1216. All that is
> necessary . . . is a finding that Honeyradio repeatedly

broadcast misleading information regarding material contest terms.[8]

In its decision, the FCC also warned broadcasters of their responsibilities for copy that is written and aired:

> Honeyradio's failure to carefully select the wording of its announcements and clues is exactly the type of conduct which leads to the broadcast of false and misleading contest programming. . . .[9]

Another significant aspect of the FCC's consideration of this case involves the agency's interest in preserving public safety and private property rights during contests.

Observing that WHNE had "received many listener complaints about trespassing treasure hunters, contest-related traffic congestion and private property damage,"[10] the Commission concluded that such a disruptive contest was inexcusable and contrary to the public interest. Clearly, station management must be mindful of such dangers during the planning stages of any contest.

The other four cases in which the FCC has assessed forfeitures involve violations of Section 509(a) of the Communications Act, the provision which makes it unlawful to fix a contest or prearrange its outcome.

Richmond, Virginia

Station WGOE was fined $2,500 in 1974 as a result of its "Right On Contest" that gave residents of certain Richmond streets an opportunity to win $1.59 gift certificates if they telephoned the station when the name of their own street was announced. After two months of this street sweeping, all winners were to become eligible to win $1,000 in merchandise on Memorial Day.

Despite the heavy promotion of the contest, the public response to it was starkly unenthusiastic. Even the advertising salesman in charge of "Right On" forgot about it by Memorial Day and was away on vacation when telephoned by other station personnel and reminded that the grand prize was to be awarded that day. The salesman did not have the $1,000 to award anyway, so he told the disc jockey on the air to reveal that one Jean Rabear had won it. Rabear, who did not even live in Virginia, let alone on a Richmond street, was a friend of the salesman.

For prearranging the outcome of the contest in direct contravention of Code Section 509(a), the station was fined for what the FCC characterized as an obvious fraud.

Further, the Commission discussed the standard to which it would hold station management in the contest area. It criticized WGOE management for its "looseness . . . that allowed . . . [the salesman] to originate and operate such a promotion without any supervision."[11] Implied again is the expectation that station management will exercise full and continuing nondelegated control and supervision over all station contests in order to assure each conforms to the law.

Bremen, Georgia

The WWCC "Turkey Shoot Contest" was broadcast ten times each day in November 1971. Listeners were urged to call the station every hour the contest ran. Accepting the first caller as that hour's contestant, the disc jockey would play a cartridge tape with twelve animal sounds. Those ranged from the barnyard noises of a pig, rooster or horse to the more exotic sounds of a camel or turkey. If the sound that came up on the tape was that of a turkey, the caller won the contest.

However, despite the station's contest advertising which led listeners to believe they had an opportunity to win each of the ten times daily the contest aired, WWCC employees determined there would be only one winner each day and so arranged the tape that only one turkey would appear daily.

For prearranging the outcome of the contest in obvious violation of Code Secton 509(a), the station was fined $3,000.

In quickly dispensing with the licensee's defense that the ownership and management of the station were personally unaware of any rigging, the FCC embraced a rule of employer-employee law and stated: "licensees are responsible for acts of their employees."[12]

Bakersfield, California

Similarly, the FCC rejected the arguments of the owner and general manager of Bakersfield station KLYD that they were unaware station manager Richard Venturino had fixed their 1968 "Win-A-Honda Contest."

While admitting that Code Section 509(a) had been breached when Venturino conspired to preselect four winners, the station insisted it should not be held responsible because neither the owner nor top management knew Venturino had done anything wrong.

The Commission explained that as long as an employee of the station, here Venturino, violated the contest statute while acting within the scope of his employment, the owner would be liable.

Imposing a $3,000 fine, the agency expressed its consternation and rationale for acting with vigor: "[T]he public . . . [was] cheated to the extent that they were deprived of an opportunity to win four of the prizes."[13]

Tampa, Florida

The last forfeiture case involves a blatant violation of Section 509(a) of the U.S. Code. Tampa station WALT conducted a "Christmas Daddy Contest" in 1966 in which listeners were told to write their names on postcards and mail them to the station. WALT announced that a grand prize drawing would then be held and one such card drawn. The prize for the winning postcard was $500.

The drawing was to be conducted by station manager Richard Oppenheimer. But before the drawing, Oppenheimer predetermined that an apparently fictitious Leroy Fisher was to win the contest. To effectuate his fraud, he ordered a station secretary to type fifty to sixty postcards with Fisher's name on them.

At noon of the last day of the contest, Oppenheimer reached into the hundreds of entries and drew out Fisher's name. There was an allegation that his excursion through the other, legitimate cards was wholly pretense and that regardless of which card was drawn, he would announce the winner's name as Fisher. At any rate, the FCC field investigation disclosed that Leroy Fisher, even if he did exist, had never personally entered the contest, and that no prize money was ever paid to anyone.

In assessing a stiff $10,000 forfeiture against WALT, the FCC expressed its outrage:

> Prearranging or predetermining the outcome of a supposedly bona fide contest with intent to deceive the public is a most serious offense. . . .[14]

NOTES/8

1. 47 U.S.C. §§ 503(b)(1)(B) and (C) (1982). See also 47 U.S.C. § 509 (1982).

2. 47 U.S.C. § 503(b)(2) (1982).

3. *Ibid.*

4. *United Broadcasting Company,* FCC 78–838, Mimeo decision 4530, at 5, November 30, 1978.

5. *Ibid.,* 3.

6. *Honeyradio, Inc.,* 69 FCC 2d 833, 834 (1978). [See also *Radio Station WHNE,* 68 FCC 2d 542 (1978) (Notice of Apparent Liability)].

7. *Ibid.,* 837.

8. *Ibid.,* 836–37.

9. *Ibid.,* 838.

10. *Ibid.,* 834.

11. *WGOE, Inc.,* et al., 49 FCC 2d 327, 354 (1974).

12. *Bremen Radio Co.,* 41 FCC 2d 595, 596 (1973). [See also *Bremen Radio Co.,* 38 FCC 2d 992 (1973) (preliminary forfeiture order)].

13. *Kern County Broadcasting Co.,* 14 FCC 2d 292, 294 (1968).

14. *Eastern Broadcasting Corp.,* 8 FCC 2d 611, 616 (1967). [See also *Eastern Broadcasting Corp.,* 10 FCC 2d 37 (1967) (petition for remission of forfeiture denied)].

CHAPTER 9

Contests for Which Stations Were Censured

The least severe sanction the FCC can impose for violations of the contest integrity rules is the censure or admonition.

Although censure implies a higher degree of reproachment, each has the same thrust: a condemnation of the contest conduct involved, an order that it be halted and a warning that it must never be repeated. The threat of a more severe sanction in the event of any recurrence is implicit.

Often, FCC admonitions direct the licensee to take immediate corrective action, such as developing a station policy to ensure contest honesty.

It is true that these lesser sanctions do not carry the often devastating economic consequences of the other penalties at the Commission's disposal. Yet, such public reprimands are embarrassing and often threaten a station's all-important public image. Note that copies of FCC letters of censure or admonition are released to the news media and the public and are published in permanent volumes for libraries across the country.

An even more immediate result of such FCC condemnation is increased Commission monitoring of daily station operations. And to a broadcast station, that specter is dreaded.

I. CENSURE

Cocoa, Florida

Seven local businesses joined with station WRKT in 1975 to sponsor a "Wild Card Contest." The contest was broadcast hourly. To win the cash prizes offered, a listener telephoned the station to correctly answer two questions: 1) how much money was in the cash call jackpot, and 2) which of fifty-two playing cards was displayed that day at one of seven participating businesses. A different business was randomly selected for each hour's contest and the total cash in the jackpot also varied throughout the weeks of the competition.

Minutes before each hour's broadcast of the contest, the disc jockey would be informed which store to announce as that hour's participant. An FCC investigation later revealed that, moments before the hour's contest was aired, WRKT's traffic manager would frequently order the business for that hour to immediately change the card displayed in its window.

As the Commission found, the result of such frantic choreography was that "[A]n unwary contestant participant had little chance of naming the right card, even if he had been in the store just minutes previously."[1]

For deceiving contestants in that way, and thereby contravening agency policy requiring contest fairness, WRKT was censured by the FCC.

Miami, Florida

The 1973 "Magnum One Contest" of WMYQ-FM offered fantastic wealth and corporate power to its winner. In fact, to use the station's own advertising language, the contest presented "the prize to end all prizes."[2]

To win, a listener had to name the cities of New York, Athens, Rome, Munich, Amsterdam, Vienna, London, Paris, Barcelona and Geneva in that order. Clues were broadcast as to the identities of the cities and the correct order.

The grand prize was advertised as the presidency and full ownership of Great American Western Corporation, a stockholding company.

In promoting the contest on air and describing the grand prize, Great American was misrepresented by WMYQ as being a part owner of General Motors, the Chase Manhattan Bank, Pan American World Airways, Hilton Hotels, The Washington Post, Boeing Aircraft, several African gold mines and the DeBeers diamond mines.

A Mrs. White won the contest and her husband, believing great wealth had been acquired, quit his job—only to learn the Great American Western Corporation was, in the words of the FCC, "no more than a shell,"[3] and worthless. The Commission discovered that the Great American holdings as broadcast were "non-existent"[4] and that the corporation "owned no stocks or other properties."[5]

WMYQ responded that it absolutely intended to purchase $10,000 worth of the various blue chip stocks for Great American once the winner was selected. In operation, Mrs. White was given the choice of the presidency of Great American as it stood (worthless) or $10,000 in cash. She took the cash.

The FCC determined that "the listening public was deceived into believing that a 'massive treasure' was actually being awarded"[6] when this announced prize was in truth a mirage.

The Commission concluded that the licensee had broadcast false, misleading, and deceptive contest advertising in violation of its 1961 Public Notice. WMYQ was strongly censured and ordered to adopt and submit a contest integrity policy to prevent future misconduct.

II. ADMONITION

Parkersburg, West Virginia

Each day for fifteen days in 1976, Parkersburg station WIBZ-FM broadcast a different secret sound. Listeners wishing to be contestants sent letters to the station identifying as many of the fifteen mystery sounds as possible. The twenty-five entries correctly identifying the most sounds were declared winners of the "Secret Sound Contest."

The WIBZ promotional advertising announced that the prizes for those twenty-five winners would be vacations for each at their choice of dream vacation spots—Las Vegas, San Juan, Fort Lauderdale or Acapulco.

Yet, some winners complained to the FCC when they discovered transportation to the vacation sites was not included. Only the hotel lodging for three nights was provided by the station. All other expenses were the personal responsibility of the winners.

WIBZ defended its conduct of the contest and argued that its description of the prizes never "implied or suggested that it included transportation or food. . . ."[7]

The FCC's decision and reasoning in resolving this case are significant in two respects.

First, while conceding that transcripts of the promos revealed

WIBZ was technically correct that the announcements had not falsely promised transportation or other expenses, the Commission nevertheless imposed liability. It concluded its 1974 Public Notice prohibiting the broadcast of misleading prize information had been violated; and it directed that a letter of admonition be sent to the station.

Second, the standard by which the advertising was to be evaluated was set as that of a reasonable person hearing the broadcast. And here, the FCC determined that the announcements describing the vacation prizes "could reasonably be construed to include transportation to the selected destination, since the prize was described as a 'vacation'. . . ."[8]

Waco, Texas

The 1974 "Love Song Contest" of station KAWA gave listeners a chance to display their song writing talents. The best original songs submitted to the station would win valuable prizes.

However, KAWA announcers and disc jockeys had incorrectly assumed—on the basis of employee conjecture around the station—that certain prizes would be awarded. Although it was an innocent misunderstanding by the announcers, incorrect prize information was in fact broadcast.

The prizes that were announced were never intended by management to be offered and many of those prizes were simply not available to be given away.

In spite of the absence of any intent to deceive the public, the FCC determined such announcements were deceptive on their face and violated the 1974 Public Notice mandating the broadcast of accurate prize information. A letter of admonishment was sent to the station.

KAWA management was also criticized in the letter for failing to more closely supervise its announcers and the on-the-air representations they made concerning the "Love Song Contest.'' Such management inattention to the day-to-day conduct of the contest was noted by the FCC as evidence of serious dereliction of the responsibility owed by every station licensee.

From this decision, it is clear that intent to deceive is not an element necessary to be proved in any action for violation of the Commission's 1974 Public Notice. And again, the heavy responsibilities of management in overseeing their employees' contest conduct are illuminated by this case.[9]

Annapolis, Maryland

A 1973 FCC investigation revealed that ''The Last Contest,'' broadcast by Annapolis station WYRE, had contravened Commission contest policy in two ways.

First, WYRE advertised that $2.3 million in prizes could be won. In truth, the maximum possible was $5,000. For that deception, the Commission ruled the station had violated its 1961 Public Notice in misleading the public by broadcasting false prize information.

Secondly, contest announcements indicated that listeners were merely to call a secret contest telephone number. The fifth or twelfth caller would be declared the winner and the only element of chance involved the listener being tuned to the station when the secret telephone number was announced.

During the several weeks of the contest, WYRE alerted listeners that the secret telephone number would be revealed on the air ''maybe tomorrow or in five days or five minutes.''[10] In truth, the number was not broadcast until the last day of the contest and the contest phone was not even connected or operational until that time.

Concluding that WYRE had broadcast false promotional announcements, the FCC determined its 1961 Public Notice requiring contest honesty had been breached.

For both violations, the station was admonished for failing

"to exercise the degree of responsibility expected of a licensee"[11] in the conduct of a broadcast contest.

Savannah, Georgia

WZAT-FM broadcast a "Last Contest" in Savannah in 1973 for which it budgeted $3,000 for any one prize package.

Yet, the station's contest advertising sparked the attention of listeners with these words:

> Building up right now in hidden vaults and secluded warehouses all over the world, a treasure so vast it would take millions of dollars to even begin to assemble it.[12]

Obviously false, the promotional announcements were faulted by the FCC as plainly having created a "misleading impression"[13] among listeners about the true value of the prizes to be awarded.

For broadcasting such deceptive matter, WZAT-FM was admonished for having contravened the Commission's 1961 Public Notice.

Philadelphia, Pennsylvania

A "Best of Broadway Contest" was aired by Philadelphia's WYSP-FM in 1972 and afforded listeners the chance to win a trip to New York City to see a Broadway musical.

Those wishing to enter the contest simply mailed postcards to the station listing their names and addresses. A station representative would then draw the winning postcard from among all those submitted; and the winner would be off to Broadway.

In this case, a WYSP disc jockey charged that Station Manager Gerald Salatino rigged the outcome by taking all entries into his private office and then emerging with the card of his father-in-law, John Regan, and proclaiming him the winner.

Within months, an FCC investigation was launched. Salatino maintained his innocence, contending the disc jockey had chosen the winning card.

The station kept no records of the contest and could not even identify the winner. In the absence of records and the inability of any other WYSP employees to remember and corroborate that father-in-law Regan had indeed been selected, the Commission decided that "there is insufficient evidence to make a determination that the winner . . . was predetermined. . . ."[14] It did conclude WYSP had not met the responsibility imposed on all broadcasters in its 1972 KOLOB Broadcasting Company, Inc. decision[15] of adequately supervising all contests to ensure they are conducted fairly.

Stymied in its efforts to ascertain the facts, the FCC admonished the station for failing to maintain detailed records of its contest. The FCC indicated that it was the responsibility of every station conducting contests to maintain complete records of contest rules, transcripts of all advertising and promotional announcements, lists of all winners and the prizes awarded.

The Commission ordered WYSP to adopt and submit a contest integrity policy which would include provisions relative to the maintenance of vital contest records.

Washington, D.C.

This is one of the few television contest cases to reach the FCC. WDCA-TV, Channel 20 in Washington, conducted a "Monkey Race Contest" in conjunction with its afternoon children's program—the "Channel 20 Club." Host Captain 20 would select postcards from those sent in by children, call their homes, and give them chances to win bikes or toys.

Recorded on video tape were actual track distance races involving competing monkeys. In all, seventeen different races were run and taped. Each young contestant selected a numbered monkey. If that monkey won the race that aired while the child waited on the phone, he or she won a prize. And several certainly did, as the station awarded 688 prizes out of 827 phone calls to young viewers.

Yet, the FCC faulted WDCA for the operation of its contest.

The station's promotional announcement that kids could win "a bike a day"[16] in the contest was criticized as being misleading to youngsters not sophisticated enough to understand that the phrase meant that there would be a maximum of only one bike winner each day. The FCC contended that children could be easily deceived by that language into believing that every lucky selection of a winning monkey would win a bicycle. That was not the case, as lesser prizes were awarded each day after one bike had been won.

The centerpiece of the Commission's reasoning was directly stated:

> In broadcasting children's contests, the licensee should be particularly careful to eliminate matter which, to a child, may be false, misleading or deceptive.[17]

The agency concluded WDCA had violated its 1961 Public Notice by broadcasting contest advertising that tended to mislead children; and directed that a letter of admonition be sent to the station.

In this case, the FCC put broadcasters on notice that if a contest is directed at children, the contest advertising will be evaluated differently. To determine whether such advertising is deceptive or misleading, the Commission will utilize a special children's standard which takes into consideration such factors as age, and lack of sophistication and discernment in advertising.

Los Angeles, California

The 1973 "Music Call Contest" of station KKDJ-FM entailed disc jockeys placing telephone calls to various listeners.

The list of names to be called each day was prepared by the KKDJ staff the day before and left overnight on the top of a desk in the studio.

Although no evidence was discovered to specifically identify the wrongdoer, someone with access to the newsroom tampered with the April 12, 1973, list and inserted the name of one Deckman at the top of the list. He would then have been the first to be telephoned the following day.

The FCC determined that prosecution for violation of the anti-fixing provisions of Section 509 of the Communications Act would be inappropriate since the guilty person could not be identified, even though the conduct certainly constituted a contravention of that law.

Instead, the Commission reprimanded KKDJ for failing to employ internal security procedures which would "guarantee the confidentiality of the list of names to be called. . . ."[18]

This decision articulates the obligation of all stations to establish and maintain strict security throughout any contest to prevent tampering or fixing.

This case also is noteworthy since it discussed the sufficiency of proof necessary to establish a violation of Section 509. Although there was evidence of prearrangement and rigging here, absent was any clue regarding the identity of the actor. As non-station personnel, presumably janitors and others, also had access to the studios overnight, and considering no one with knowledge came forward to testify, identifying the individual became nearly impossible.

Without such an identification, the FCC was unwilling to proceed with Section 509 charges; and opted instead for the reprimand sanction.

Kaukauna, Wisconsin

Station WKAU broadcast a "Listen To The Music Contest" in 1973 in which portions of three different records were spliced together and then aired. Contestants were required to correctly identify the individual songs and artists from the jumbled version to win record albums as prizes.

But a common problem developed during the early days of the contest. Eight or ten young listeners, eager to win albums, quickly called the station, often with correct answers. They monopolized the game each hour.

Although the announced contest rules had not precluded such frequent calls, the WKAU program director and disc jockeys devised a plan to combat the obnoxious repeat contestants.

The disc jockeys explained to those children who called with an answer that they could play but once a day, although this rule was not announced over the air. Too, if a disc jockey had announced that the fourth caller with the correct answer would win and it developed that the fourth caller was one of those eight or ten children, the DJ would deliberately misrepresent the truth and inform the child that he or she was not the fourth caller and instead take the next call.

The station was admonished by the FCC for changing the contest rules without apprising the listening public and for improperly disqualifying certain callers by refusing to let them compete. The Commission characterized this as a failure to conduct the contest either fairly or as the station's advertising had represented to the public it would be conducted, thus contravening Commission policy as set out in the KOLOB Broadcasting Co. decision.[19]

Philadelphia, Pennsylvania

A 1971 contest broadcast over WHAT-AM, Philadelphia, offered a scholarship to the Career Academy School of Broadcasting as the grand prize. But no winner was ever selected and all three finalists were told they'd have to pay up to $2,000 to attend the broadcasting school.

Although WHAT had lent its name and that of one of its personalities to the contest, and the contest was advertised heavily on the station, it was decidedly not a station-sponsored or station-produced contest. The contest was independently conducted by the broadcasting school which was solely responsible for the selection of the winners. For that reason, the FCC concluded that WHAT had "not intentionally broadcast a fraudulent contest"[20] and abstained from meting out any of the more severe sanctions against the station.

The Commission did, however, reprimand WHAT for failing "to properly supervise the contest to ensure that Career Academy selected a winner. . . ."[21] It ordered the broadcaster to adopt a contest integrity policy to prevent future misconduct and submit it to the FCC.

Explicit in this decision is the obligation of each station to guarantee the integrity of all contests which are broadcast in association with the station, even though a particular contest is neither produced nor conducted by the station.

NOTES/9

1. *Bucks County Radio News, Inc.*, 61 FCC 2d 1091, 1092 (1976).

2. *Bartell Broadcasting of Florida, Inc.*, 51 FCC 2d 2, 6 (1974).

3. *Ibid.*, 5.

4. *Ibid.*, 3.

5. *Ibid.*, 4.

6. *Ibid.*, 5.

7. *Randy Jay Broadcasting Company, 64 FCC 2d 1121 (1977)*.

8. *Ibid.*, 1122.

9. *Centrum Corp.*, 36 Rad. Reg.2d 201 (1976).

10. *Radio Chesapeake, Inc.*, 29 Rad. Reg.2d 1371, 1372 (1974).

11. *Ibid.* 1373.

12. *Weis Broadcasting Company*, 45 FCC 2d 536, 537 (1974).

13. *Ibid.*

14. *SJR Communications, Inc.*, 45 FCC 2d 928, 930 (1974).

15. *KOLOB Broadcasting Company, Inc.*, 36 FCC 2d 586, 587 (1972).

16. *Channel 20, Incorporated*, 43 FCC 2d 1075, 1077 (1973).

17. *Ibid.* 1078.

18. *Pacific and Southern Company, Inc.*, 44 FCC 2d 629 (1973).

19. *Fox River Communications, Inc.*, 45 FCC 2d 1081, 1082 (1974).

20. *Independence Broadcasting Co., Inc.*, et al., 53 FCC 2d 1161, 1167 (1975).

21. *Ibid.*

CHAPTER 10

Contests Which Resulted in License Renewals and Transfers of Ownership

In several contest cases, the FCC has rendered decisions which cannot technically be described as constituting sanctions against the stations involved. Yet, many broadcasters have been seriously penalized and others have indirectly lost their licenses in these cases. This chapter's first focus is on license renewals.

With respect to renewals, the several cases which follow represent victories for the broadcasters charged with contest misconduct. Licenses on the block, facing revocation, short-term renewal, forfeiture or admonition, these stations were successful in winning license renewal. However, several of these victories were hollow because the FCC renewed the licenses only to allow the beleaguered station owner to sell. In that way, the Commission avoided the need to determine the merits of the pending contest allegations. Too, some licenses were renewed subject to certain conditions, including requiring the licensee to adopt station contest integrity guidelines.

The procedural context should be noted.[1] The cases which follow largely involve existing, licensed stations applying to the FCC for the periodic renewal of license. Either of two contest developments will, at least temporarily, block the licensee's road to renewal of its license.

First, a local viewer, listener or citizens group could file a complaint with the Commission which alleges contest violations that present "substantial and material"[2] questions of fact. Second, the FCC itself, on the basis of its review of the station's record and any contest charges, could be in doubt as to whether license renewal is warranted.

In either case, the agency will designate the renewal application for hearing[3] and specify the contest allegations as issues to be probed at the hearing. At the conclusion of that proceeding, the presiding Administrative Law Judge will render a decision regarding renewal. The Commission will then review that decision and either affirm or overrule it.

The other procedural context for the cases in this chapter involves the Communications Act requirement that station licensees must obtain FCC approval before selling their stations.[4] The Commission determines the appropriateness of the transfer based on whether the proposed purchaser possesses all qualifications of a Commission licensee and would operate the station in the public interest.

Los Angeles, California

The license of KNBC-TV, the Los Angeles station owned and operated by the NBC Television Network, was jeopardized by network broadcasts of the popular game show "Hollywood Squares."

Premiering in 1966, "Squares" boxed nine celebrities in a giant size tic-tac-toe board. When a question was propounded by emcee Peter Marshall, the celebrity had the option of correctly answering or bluffing. Contestants from the audience won squares, prizes, and money by either correctly agreeing or disagreeing with the celebrity's answer.

The show, propelled by flashing lights around each square, sirens, buzzers, and frequent humorous celebrity responses from the likes of Paul Lynde and Charlie Weaver, shot to the top of the ratings. The FCC put KNBC's license on the block when it was revealed the show was also propelled by behind-the-scenes coaching of the celebrities to help them prepare their answers and ad libs.

Two Commission decisions were rendered. The first, in 1968, was based on the results of a staff field inquiry which indicated numerous celebrities were given the questions and often suggested answers before the shows were taped.

Although it was noted NBC ran visual caveats across the screen, namely: "celebrity panelists are briefed in advance,"[5] the FCC decided the viewers remained naive of the extent to which the celebrities were woodshedded. As the decision read, such failure to come forward and clarify the true help given the celebrities "led them [the public] falsely to believe that the guest celebrities had no foreknowledge of the questions they were attempting to answer."[6]

The FCC acknowledged that NBC and the program's independent producer—Heatter-Quigley, Inc.—had not violated Section 509 of the Communications Act because the Act makes it unlawful to secretly supply *contestants* with answers in advance. The government frankly admitted that the "Squares" celebrities were not really the contestants, but nonetheless concluded "the public has . . . been misled. . . ."[7]

The Commission characterized the visual advisory as inadequate and the network's contest integrity procedures as "lax."[8] In its admonition, the FCC directed NBC to revise its contest and quiz show procedures and report such revisions to the Commission for consideration in conjunction with KNBC's license renewal.

The second decision, reached in 1970, turned on two intervening developments. By the time of this decision, NBC was broadcasting a new disclaimer on "Hollywood Squares:"

> Areas of questions designed for each celebrity and possible
> bluff answers are discussed with each celebrity in advance.
> In the course of their briefing, actual questions and answers
> may be given or discerned by the celebrities.[9]

NBC had also adopted what the FCC considered "voluminous"[10] and "detailed"[11] contest and quiz integrity guidelines. The new standards included provisions requiring increased supervision by the network of contests that are produced by independent programming sources outside the network. The revised and strengthened procedures, designed to eliminate any public deception about contest operations, satisfied the Commission.

Concluding that the new integrity guidelines would force future "compliance by NBC of its responsibilities in this area,"[12] the FCC renewed KNBC's license.

In this decision, the FCC imposed direct responsibility on broadcasters to supervise even independently-produced, non-station or non-network programs to ensure the public is not misled.

And again in this case, it should be noted that the FCC took action even though the contest conduct in question did not technically violate Section 509. It should be remembered that the Commission has penalized broadcasters on other occasions despite the strict statutory lawfulness of the contest involved. Broadcasters should be on notice that if the FCC is sufficiently offended by certain contest conduct, it will root around until it finds some way to reach that conduct and hold the broadcaster accountable.

Jacksonville, Florida

The license of Jacksonville station WPDQ was designated for hearing by the FCC when it was discovered that two station employees had rigged the outcome of a 1967 contest. The "Thank You Contest" involved station disc jockeys selecting the names of area residents at random from the phone book. A name would be read by the announcer and that person would win part of the $60,000 grand prize if he or she telephoned the station within the time limit.

WPDQ's troubles began when a disc jockey and the station's program director conspired with others to rig the contest one day. An accomplice, one Youngblood, was recruited and told his name would be broadcast on September 4, 1967, when the day's prize was a new car. Youngblood made the timely call to the station, he was awarded the car, quickly sold it by prearrangement for $3,500, and divided the money among the co-conspirators.

The winner was allowed to keep only $400 with which to pay his income tax. The elaborate scheme unravelled when Youngblood, upon reflection, decided his cut was too small. When the others would not meet his demands for more money he went public with the story.[13]

When Henderson Belk, the owner and president of WPDQ, was first informed of the allegations, he ordered his attorney to conduct an immediate and full investigation of the charges. At the conclusion of the inquiry, he fired the disc jockey involved. The program director had already left the station. Belk then sent a complete copy of the investigative report to the FCC.

The Commission set the license down for hearing. At issue was whether that admitted prearrangement of the contest outcome, in obvious violation of Section 509 of the Act, warranted the imposition of a penalty.

While acknowledging that "serious misconduct did in fact

occur,''[14] the FCC renewed the license for the full license term. The license was saved by the quick and decisive management action. Noted the decision:

> (O)nce Belk was apprised that there may have been misconduct . . . he took prompt, effective measures to . . . prevent any recurrence, including firing the station personnel involved, ceasing the big prize contests. . . .[15]

The Commission emphasized that had Belk not taken such ''stringent measures, . . . the facts here adduced would have had serious implications as to the licensee's qualifications to remain a licensee of the Commission.''[16]

A critical factor indeed in this case was that the licensee himself alerted the FCC to the contest wrongdoing.

This decision provides solid advice to any broadcaster caught in a contest crisis in the future:

1) Quickly investigate any allegations of contest impropriety;

2) Ensure the credibility and exhaustiveness of the inquiry by selecting an attorney to conduct it;

3) Act decisively to punish proven wrongdoing;

4) Take steps to eliminate its recurrence; and

5) Be the first to apprise the FCC of the problem.

Cleveland, Ohio

The ''Million Dollar Contest'' broadcast in 1967 by NBC's owned-and-operated radio station in Cleveland—WKYC—threatened that station's license renewal.

WKYC recorded the serial numbers of 1,000 one dollar bills and then distributed them throughout the Cleveland area. The station later broadcast two serial numbers each hour of the day. To win, a listener holding one of the bills had to telephone the station within eleven minutes and then take the bill to the studio. $1,000 was to be awarded for each winning bill redeemed.

Using WKYC's calculations, the total that could be won was $1 million. (1,000 $1 bills × $1,000 for each redeemed). It promoted its contest with ads which read: "WKYC, in a contest to end all contests, offers $1 million cash to listeners."[17]

Yet, there was only one winner during the four weeks of the contest; and the station paid only $1,000 in prize money.

The FCC criticized the contest as being nearly impossible to win and charged that the promotional ads "tended to mislead the public in that they contained extravagant claims concerning the amount of money to be given away."[18]

Characterizing the odds against any listener winning such a contest given the sea of bills already in circulation in Cleveland as "far greater than a billion to one,"[19] the Commission concluded the ads, while "not technically false . . . were deceptive and misleading in their implications since the chances . . . [of winning were so] extremely remote."[20]

Admonishing the station that it considered the contest promotion to have been misleading and deceptive, and thereby violating the 1961 Public Notice, the FCC reserved until the time WKYC filed its application for renewal of its license the question of whether these violations should prevent such renewal.

However, that point never came because in the interim NBC received Commission approval to sell WKYC to a local Ohio corporation.[21] The question of what sanction this contest deception would have sparked in a renewal proceeding remains unanswered.

It is clear, however, that contests heavily promoted with extravagant prize claims but with little inherent chances of listeners or viewers winning those grandiose prizes will be actionable even though the language employed is not technically false.

Hollywood, Florida

"Twenty-One," the notorious 1950s quiz show that was forced off network television amid charges of rigging and fixing, was produced by Jack Barry and Dan Enright. Barry, in fact, had been the program's emcee. Wise investors both, Barry and Enright purchased a Florida radio station with some of their broadcasting riches.

When that station, WGMA, applied to the FCC for license renewal, it set in motion a series of decisions and appeals that eventually forced the co-owners to sell their interests in the station.

In 1962, the Commission designated the renewal application for hearing. The issue was whether, given the involvement of those co-owners in the production of fixed TV quiz shows, they possessed "the requisite qualifications to be a licensee of the Commission."[22]

After that hearing, the Commission voted in 1964 to strip WGMA of its license because its owners had shown a "propensity for deception"[23] in broadcasting. Seeking to put their conduct into perspective, Barry and Enright argued that because the rigging of quiz shows had been "prevalent throughout the industry,"[24] their station's license should be renewed. The FCC's retort was that it didn't "consider misconduct which constitutes a fraud upon the public to be any less serious because . . . [it is] widespread."[25]

Addressing the wreckage of "Twenty-One" and its national impact, the opinion concluded:

> The prolonged deception [of the show's viewers] . . . by Enright, with at least the knowledge and acquiescence of Barry, is so patently and flagrantly contrary to the public interest. . . .[26] [that it warrants revocation of license for any station they own.]

It is interesting to note that neither Barry nor Enright had technically violated any law. After all, it was only *after* "Twenty-One" and the quiz scandals that the Congress quickly amended the statutes to make any further quiz or contest rigging unlawful.

Even so, the FCC considered the WGMA license tainted with the quiz scandals and its owners unfit to serve as licensees. The Commission reasoned that since Barry and Enright had a track record of violating the public trust on their national TV program, they couldn't be trusted to operate their Florida radio station in the public interest.

Regardless of the fact that the 1964 FCC decision was wrapped in the indignation the public so keenly felt at the quiz scandals, the Commission's revocation decision was overturned in 1965 by the U.S. Court of Appeals.[27]

The Appeals Court rebuked the FCC for attaching such a severe penalty to the noncriminal conduct of Barry and Enright. The Court particularly faulted the inconsistencies in other FCC quiz scandal decisions. The Court noted an NBC owned-and-operated station had been granted license renewal even though its owners, the NBC television network, had also played a "role in the deceptive quiz shows"[28] which aired on that network.

On remand to the agency in 1966, the Commissioners still bristled at the idea of renewing the WGMA license: "[W]e are not inclined to take any action that might be construed as condoning the misconduct of Enright and Barry."[29] Yet, the FCC acknowledged that "the applicant here was guilty of violating only our sense of propriety and ethics"[30] and therefore, consistent with the opinion of the appellate court, shouldn't be penalized more than other stations which at times violate criminal statutes and yet are granted renewals of license.

The Commission granted WGMA a one-year renewal of license on the condition that Enright and Barry divest themselves of all ownership interest within sixty days and sell the station to a qualified applicant.

Chairman E. William Henry, in a vigorous dissent, argued

that the courts and agency had been too soft on Barry and Enright. He felt that they had shocked, disillusioned and duped millions of Americans and scarred the reputation of all television broadcasting. He therefore argued that the only appropriate decision would be to deny license renewal and force the station off the air so Barry and Enright wouldn't have any interest to sell to anyone.[31]

One stark factor distinguishes this case from most other typical station contest or quiz fact situations, and thereby limits to these facts the impact of the Appeals Court's reversal. Here, the misconduct of Barry and Enright occurred in connection with their production of network television quiz programs hundreds of miles away from Florida and WGMA. Their quiz improprieties did not involve WGMA at all. WGMA, a sideline investment of the two, didn't even broadcast any of their rigged quiz shows.

The most typical factual context in which the FCC prosecutes today involves sanctioning a station owner for contest improprieties in connection with a contest that has been broadcast on that owner's station. Given that fact, FCC contest penalties imposed on other stations would not likely be reversed today nor run afoul of the Appeals Court's WGMA decision.

Columbia, South Carolina

When Columbia station WOIC sought renewal of its license in 1969, a local black civic group filed a petition to deny with the FCC.[32]

The complaint alleged that Tampa, Florida, station WTMP, also owned by WOIC principal Joseph Speidel III, had been involved in contest improprieties. Specifically, it was claimed that the "Mr. and Mrs. Soul Night Contest" broadcast on WTMP had been fraudulent. The argument was that the $1,150 raised for minority scholarship funds at area colleges during the contest had been spent instead to repair and remodel WTMP's office suites, and that nothing "was ever donated to any scholarship fund."[33]

Rather than refute the charges, WOIC ignored them as irrelevant to the renewal of its own license since the contest complained of was broadcast on another station.

The FCC disagreed and found the charges serious enough to designate the license renewal for hearing on whether the "Soul Night Contest" had worked a "deception upon the public."[34]

Before the hearing commenced, WOIC filed a lengthy pleading responding in detail to the charges. It also filed an application seeking Commission approval of its sale to a local black corporation, Nuance.

WOIC's detailed factual rebuttal contained evidence that, albeit delayed, all the contest proceeds were eventually paid out to the colleges involved. Further, the FCC was assured that none of the contest money raised was ever used to remodel or rebuild the WTMP studios.

The Commission was satisfied by the WOIC rebuttal and concluded it had erased the "substantial questions of fact requiring a hearing."[35]

The FCC terminated the hearing, and renewed the license on the condition that the transfer of ownership be effected. The agency then formally approved the application of WOIC, Inc. to assign its license to Nuance.[36]

This decision indicates the willingness of the FCC to hold one station's license hostage, indeed to designate it for hearing, upon allegations of contest misconduct at a totally separate and geographically distant station under common ownership. The advice to stations so situated and similarly attacked at renewal time is to always mount a full defense to any charges of contest irregularities because the FCC regards those issues as vital and uniformly worthy of its scrutiny.[37]

Slidell, Louisiana

Slidell station WVSL-FM played progressive jazz and rock music exclusively. The acting station manager, with neither the approval nor knowledge of the station's owners, developed and broadcast a "Mother Radio Contest" in 1973.

Listeners would enter the contest at local record stores by voting and registering their preference for either the jazz or rock music that WVSL played. From those ballots, names of winners were to be drawn and awarded prizes which included cruises to the Bahamas and ten-speed bicycles.

But as soon as the owners discovered the unauthorized contest was being conducted, they immediately fired the employees involved in it. When those disgruntled employees left, they destroyed all the entries that had been received. The station subsequently did nothing about the contest. Thereafter, thirty-three area listeners wrote the FCC complaining that the prizes had not been awarded.

Upon being informed of the inability of WVSL to award prizes without any contest entries from which to choose, the FCC refused to penalize the station. It even rejected as unnecessary WVSL's offer to conduct another similar contest from the beginning. That decision was based on the fact that the station had already discontinued its jazz/rock format and re-running such a music preference contest would have been irrelevant and "inappropriate."[38]

During this controversy, WVSL's financial status deteriorated and its principal stockholder became quite ill. So, the licensee corporation sought Commission permission to sell the station to another corporation. The agency approved that assignment of license.

The impact of this decision is that allegations of contest improprieties, specifically the refusal to award announced prizes, will not warrant denial of license assignment or other penalties when a factual impossibility not the result of the licensee's own acts or omissions prevents certain contest performance.

The FCC's decision-making involving contests is not limited to licensing cases. The chapters which follow focus in on the other specific limitations the law imposes on contest broadcasts and the FCC decisions which have interpreted them.

NOTES/10

1. See Chapter 4, note 6, and the accompanying textual material.

2. 47 U.S.C. § 309(e) (1982).

3. *Ibid.*

4. 47 U.S.C. § 310(d) (1982).

5. *Quiz Program Practices,* 14 FCC 2d 976, 977 (1968).

6. *Ibid.,* 976.

7. *Ibid.,* 977.

8. *Ibid.*

9. Roth, "The Quizzes and the Law," 3 *Performing Arts Review* 629, 638 (1972).

10. *National Broadcasting Co., Inc.,* 25 FCC 2d 106, 107 (1970).

11. *Ibid.*

12. *Ibid.*

13. *Belk Broadcasting Co. of Florida, Inc.,* 42 FCC 2d 851 (1972). [Initial Decision of Hearing Examiner Chester F. Naumowicz, Jr.]

14. *Belk Broadcasting Co. of Florida, Inc.,* 42 FCC 2d 844, 849 (1973).

15. *Ibid.,* 848.

16. *Ibid.,* 849.

17. *In Re Complaint Concerning Deceptive Advertising by Station WKYC, Cleveland, Ohio,* 14 FCC 2d 683, 684 (1968).

18. *Ibid.*

19. *Ibid.*

20. *Ibid.*

21. *National Broadcasting Company, Inc.,* et al., 38 FCC 2d 65 (1972). It should be noted that NBC sought assignment of WKYC-AM and FM to Ohio Communications, Inc., in order to comply with the FCC's multiple ownership rules then in force which limited its holdings in any given locality. (NBC already owned a television station in Cleveland and was therefore at its maximum ownership level with that one station.)

22. *Melody Music, Inc.,* 44 FCC 2714, 2715 (1962).

23. *Melody Music, Inc.,* 36 FCC 701, 706 (1964).

24. *Ibid.*

25. *Ibid.*

26. *Ibid.,* 705

27. *Melody Music, Inc. v. FCC,* 345 F.2d 730 (D.C. Cir. 1965).

28. *Ibid.,* 732.

29. *Melody Music, Inc.,* 2 FCC 2d 958, 962 (1966).

30. *Ibid.*

31. *Ibid.,* pp. 964–969. It could be argued that one way to distinguish the FCC's renewal of the NBC-owned stations was that NBC had not participated in the rigging nor had actual knowledge that certain programs were being fixed. On the other hand, Barry and Enright had participated or acquiesced in the rigging and knew their programs were fixed.

32. *WOIC, Inc.,* 39 FCC 2d 355 (1973).

33. *Ibid.,* 369.

34. *Ibid.,* 370, note 30.

35. *WOIC, Inc.,* 44 FCC 2d 891, 892 (1974).

36. *Ibid.,* 894.

37. The question of whether the FCC could have imposed short-term

renewal or revocation sanctions on WOIC given the D.C. Circuit's 1965 Melody Music decision, *supra* note 27, is rather academic considering no sanction was imposed here. Yet, the factor distinguishing the two cases is that here the prior misconduct allegedly occurred at another radio station owned and controlled by the licensee and was related to station operations; whereas in *Melody Music,* the prior misconduct occurred during the independent production of network quiz shows and was not related to station operations.

It is nonetheless provocative to consider what impact *Melody Music* would have had on a Commission decision here, for instance, to deny renewal of license to WOIC at the conclusion of the aborted hearing. For, punishing WOIC (the scene of no improprieties) for the misconduct of its owner allegedly perpetrated at distant WTMP is logically not significantly different from sanctioning WGMA (similarly, the scene of no improprieties) with license revocation for the misconduct of its owners at the distant network production level.

38. *Mid-South Broadcasters Corporation,* 44 FCC 2d 979, 980 (1973).

CHAPTER 11

Petitions to Amend the FCC's Contest Rules and Regulations

The federal Administrative Procedure Act confers upon interested individuals the right to petition government agencies to amend agency rules and regulations.[1]

On two separate occasions, citizens have petitioned the FCC to extend the scope of its contest integrity rules. Neither petition was granted.

The Geller Petition

Henry Geller, a former FCC General Counsel and nationally-recognized communications law activist, filed a petition requesting that the Commission actually ban contests which can be won on the basis of mindless chance rather than skill. He contended that the only legitimate contests are those in which the listener's or viewer's skill determines the outcome.[2]

Geller took aim at those contests which award prizes on the basis of chance or luck, as when a listener happens to win by fortuitously tuning into the station when the amount in the cash call jackpot is announced. He protested that those amounted to nothing less than bribing listeners into selecting particular stations.

The Commission flatly denied the petition and rejected Geller's reasoning. The opinion emphasized that the record contained no evidence that such contests harmed the public in any way. And absent such a showing that those non-skill contests violated the licensee's obligation to operate in the public interest, the FCC refused to extend its contest rules.[3]

This decision allows stations to select whatever type of contest they wish, without federal limitation. The Commission's inquiry remains limited to whether a station conducted or advertised a contest deceptively, rather than whether a station exercised reasonable judgment in selecting the type of contest to hold—skill, non-skill, chance, luck of a drawing, sixth caller, first postmark, etc. The programming decision is the licensee's. The FCC will then police the execution of the contest chosen rather than, by the rule recommended by Geller, prohibit certain types of contests and thereby limit the ability of individual stations to choose their own contests.

The significance of this rejection of the Geller proposal is in the contest latitude the Commission insures will remain with each station.

The Rodeo Petition

In a somewhat lighter vein, although the proponents were no doubt dead serious, was the petition filed by the Humane Society of the United States. It sought a rule prohibiting the broadcast of rodeos. Alternately, it requested a broadcast disclosure that rodeos are rigged in that the animals are artificially forced to act wildly and dangerously.

The argument of the society was that the public is routinely deceived by rodeos—which by definition are contests between rider and animal. The organization protested that the viewing public is misled as to the true nature of the contest and its competitors; specifically, that unbeknownst to the public "cruel methods are employed to trigger the 'wild' behavior"[4] of the animals.

Although one member of the Commission agreed that this alleged rodeo deception was comparable to that conduct prohibited in rigged quiz show contests, his position attracted no concurrence and was relegated to a lone dissent.

The Commission majority noted its quiz show and contest integrity rules are "requirements which deal with contests for people, not livestock, and involve intellectual contests, not physical skill."[5] It refused to extend those rules to contests between man and beast or to physical skills contests.

NOTES/11

1. 5 U.S.C. § 553(e) (1982).

2. *Broadcast of Station Contests,* 37 Rad. Reg.2d 260 (1976).

3. *Ibid.* 261.

4. *Rodeo Programming,* 61 FCC 2d 934, 935 (1976).

5. *Ibid.* 936.

CHAPTER 12

Broadcasting the Contestant's Voice: What the FCC Requires

I. THE LAW

Even if a station's contest, game or promotion is lawful in every respect and conducted well within the FCC's parameters, a broadcaster may nonetheless face legal liability if a contestant's voice is improperly broadcast.

Such liability can take either or both of two forms: lawsuits by the contestant for invasion of privacy or sanctions by the FCC for violation of its rule forbidding such broadcasts in certain circumstances.

Those situations covered by the FCC rule will be examined first, as they are far more typical. Civil suits for invasion of privacy are discussed in the next chapter.

Only those stations airing certain types of contests need be alert to this legal pitfall. The contests relevant here would include those in which a disc jockey selects names at random from a phone book and places calls to those individuals to engage them in a contest on the air. Even if the station telephoned listeners or viewers who had themselves mailed in postcards with their names, addresses and phone numbers, and subsequently aired a portion of the conversation between the station and the contestant, it could still be hit with a sizeable penalty.

Whether the contest be a "Cash Call Jackpot" or one in which the lucky postcard drawn from a drum of entries is given a chance to play a game on the air, whenever the telephone is a part of the contest in any way, broadcasters must be careful and conduct the contest with the additional requirements of this chapter in mind.

Particularly, dangers are involved when the telephone call is originated by the station. Which is not to say that phone contests are to be avoided because, in operation, they're characterized by an immediacy and excitement that attracts listeners. But care and strict adherence to an additional FCC rule are required whenever a contestant's voice is broadcast (either live, simultaneously with the call on the air or on a tape delay basis) as part of a contest.

The bottom line is this: *before* either recording a telephone conversation with a contestant for later broadcast or broadcasting such a conversation simultaneously, the licensee must inform the party of the station's intention to broadcast all or part of the conversation. This rule, (73.1206, commonly known as the notification requirement)[1], was adopted by the FCC in 1970[2] in order to allow those people whose telephone conversations were to be either recorded or broadcast the option of refusing a broadcast station such permission.

Unless the contestant's consent is received prior to the taping and broadcasting, the conversation may not be used on the air as part of the contest. Nor can it be used even as part of a subsequent promotion airing the shrieks of joy recorded when a lucky listener was awarded some attractive prize.

Typically, this requirement can be met by the disc jockey using the following language when the listener answers his or her phone:

> HELLO, MRS. JONES. THIS IS _____ FROM WXYZ RADIO. WE'D LIKE TO PLAY OUR "CASH CALL JACKPOT" WITH YOU THIS MORNING. WE PLAN TO BROADCAST OUR CONVERSATION ON THE AIR TO GIVE OUR LISTENERS A CHANCE TO HEAR HOW YOU DO AND WHAT YOU WIN. IS THAT AGREEABLE TO YOU?

To protect itself, the station should record the disc jockey's request as read and the contestant's response. If the response is affirmative, the game may begin and all or part of it broadcast live or tape-delayed. A suggested segue to be used by the on-air personality after so notifying the contestant:

> WE'VE GOT MRS. JONES ON THE LINE AND SHE'S READY TO PLAY THE "CASH CALL JACKPOT" CONTEST.

The tape of each notification should be retained by the station on a special reel containing all other notifications as conclusive evidence of compliance with the rule.

With respect to contests, there is only one exception to the notification requirement. If the listener originates the call as part of a contest and the game or program customarily broadcasts telephone conversations, the caller will be presumed to be on notice that it is likely the call will be aired.

In its decision adopting this rule and its implied consent exception, the Commission provided only one example of what it considered the type of program a listener might call and be presumed to know of the likelihood of the call being aired: an open mike call-in telephone show. The Commission was silent on contest exceptions.

While the FCC would be hard-pressed to distinguish between a call-in phone show and a contest in which the sixth caller wins a ticket to some concert, the agency's actions are not always predictable or symmetrically logical. Suffice it to report the Commission has not been faced with such a case and so has not to date ruled on the question. However, it would appear that such a contest—if the caller was aware that the calls of other contestants had been broadcast on other occasions—would fit nicely within the exception and the disc jockey would be under no obligation to read the caller the notification language before broadcasting the conversation.

II. THE HISTORICAL PERSPECTIVE

The current FCC rules limiting the broadcasting of telephone conversations, and the watchful and concerned regulatory attitude of the Commission today can be explained by briefly consulting the historical development of the relevant policy issues since 1947.

As a result of FCC decisions rendered in 1947 and 1948, an audible "beep tone" was required whenever a licensee recorded a telephone conversation with a contestant.[3] The beep tone requirement was imposed because the Commission was "keenly appreciative of the importance and desirability of privacy in telephone conversation"[4] and determined they "should be free from any listening-in by others that is not done with the knowledge and authorization of the parties to the call. . . ."[5]

That rationale, the predicate for the public policy favoring privacy of phone converations, remains vigorous today and underpins the notice requirements of Rule 73.1206. Only the means of alerting the contestant have changed. In 1948, a beep tone put the listener on notice. Today, the disc jockey verbally advises the contestant of the station's intent to broadcast the call.

For twenty-five years, the beep tone had done the job, earned its place in broadcasting and "become recognized throughout the United States"[6] as the warning to callers that their conversations were being recorded by the station.

In a 1972 decision,[7] the FCC eliminated the beep tone requirement for broadcast stations which thereafter strictly adhered to the notice provisions of Section 73.1206.

Throughout the years since 1947 and extending through today, the perspective operative at the FCC in this area has been that of the individual listener or viewer who has been called on the phone by a station. In a stern public notice to broadcasters in 1966, the government acknowledged having received numerous complaints from the public concerning broadcast contests.[8] The FCC noted the various ways in which some contests had offended the public, including those in which the listeners' rights to privacy were invaded, they were annoyed at home by the calls, or were somehow exposed to embarrassment. The Commission warned broadcasters that any contests which had such adverse impact on the rights of listeners or viewers evidenced licensee irresponsibility and would not be tolerated.

Six years later, the FCC issued another formal notice to the broadcasting industry which emphasized the agency's continuing concern over phone call improprieties and which escalated the reproachment of the industry.[9] Several violations of the Section 73.1206 requirements were reported by the Commission, including some in which disc jockeys had made calls on the air designed to elicit funny and entertaining responses from the unwary victims while the listening audience was regaled by the practical joke.

Offended by such assaults on the rights of listeners toward whom it had attempted to sensitize stations, the FCC toughened its stand by alerting broadcasters that such phone calls could result in not only punishment for violating Section 73.1206, but also various state and federal telephone regulations prohibiting the use of phones "to frighten, abuse, torment, or harass another,"[10] and even Section 223 of the Communications Act which makes it a criminal offense to use the phone to annoy or harass another person.[11]

And broadcasters who have violated the FCC's phone contest rules have felt the agency's wrath in a series of cases. An examination of those decisions will reveal precisely what contest conduct is to be avoided by broadcast stations.

III. SUMMARY OF PHONE CONTEST DECISIONS

The FCC has decided eight cases involving allegations of Rule 73.1206 violations since 1972. In six of them, broadcasters were found to have violated the rule; and the penalties imposed ranged from forfeitures to letters of warning. In two cases, the Commission found the stations involved innocent of any phone call wrongdoing. No licenses have ever been revoked or short-term renewals attached due to 73.1206 violations. The most severe sanction imposed to date has been the forfeiture.

Forfeitures

Pittsburgh, Pennsylvania

A $2,000 fine was assessed against Pittsburgh station WKTQ in 1975 for phone contest improprieties. The stations's "Cash Call" contest involved a disc jockey calling area phone numbers at random. If the person answered "I listen to the new sound of 13 Q,"[12] the deejay then informed the party that the conversation was being broadcast live and that the person had won a prize.

The FCC found this practice violated the advance notice requirements of the Rule. The station argued that the mere use of that phrase in answering the telephone did not constitute a conversation by definition and therefore did not trigger the notice requirement. [Note: the Rule obligates stations to notify persons whose "telephone conversations"[13] the station intends to broadcast or tape.]

The Commission retorted that even the word "hello" was a conversation within the meaning of the Rule and that the plain language of 73.1206 required the station to notify the party called before broadcasting even one word from that phone contestant's mouth.

For having failed to so notify the contestant in this situation until after eight words had been spoken and simultaneously aired, the FCC fined WKTQ $2,000.

This decision certainly renders this type of contest inoperative. Too, the case crisply evidences the agency's strictness in this area. The message is clear: before airing a single word from a phone contestant, the station must advise that contestant of its intent to air the conversation. Of course, deejays are not precluded from carrying on even lengthy conversations off-the-air and which are not being recorded for later broadcast.[14] For example:

CONTESTANT: (answering telephone) "Hello . . ."
D.J.:   "This is _____ from WXYZ Radio. How are you this morning? Would you like to play the 'Cash Call Contest' with me today?"
CONTESTANT: "Sure, what do I need to do to win?"
D.J.:   "Well, just tell me how much is in WXYZ's 'Cash Call' jackpot this hour. But first, I want you to know that in a second I want to go on the air with you to play the game, to broadcast our conversation on the air to give our listeners a chance to hear how you do and what you win. Is that agreeable to you?"

If the contestant's response is affirmative, it is at that moment only that the deejay can broadcast the conversation live or even record it for later broadcast. Up until that point, the conversation is a private one between two parties. The rest of it can be made public only with the consent of the contestant.

Beaumont, Texas

In 1974, the FCC ordered Beaumont station KTLI to pay a $20,000 fine for violating Section 73.1206. Veteran morning disc jockey Gordon Baxter, who frequently made calls to rival radio stations and broadcast the often funny exchanges live, on this occasion telephoned one B. B. Healan—the general manager of competitor KTRM. Baxter queried Healan on the air about the rumor Healan had been spreading that Baxter was facing imminent retirement. The two engaged in what was at times a rather humorous dialogue.

In the finest competitive spirit, Healan subsequently expressed surprise that the conversation had been broadcast, asserted Baxter had not so advised him, and fired off a complaint to the FCC blowing the whistle on his old friend.

Baxter, while admitting that he didn't recall formally notifying Healan that the call was being aired, remarked that he "would swear he [Healan] knew it from his every word and manner."[15] Baxter was referring to the fact that during the conversation, both he and Healan had been speaking in their "broadcast voices."

It was KTLI's position that this case fell within the exception to the notice requirement, namely that no formal notice need be given if the other party on the phone can be presumed to be aware that the call is being broadcast. KTLI argued that Healan knew Baxter made and simultaneously aired such calls to rivals and that Healan had spoken with his on-air voice, thereby indicating his awareness.

The FCC rejected that analysis and ruled that awareness can be presumed only if 1) the other party originates the call; and 2) it is obvious to them that such calls are customarily broadcast. As KTLI's Baxter had originated the call, such a presumption was unavailable to his station. The awareness presumption exception therefore not being applicable, Baxter was required by the Rule to give formal notice to Healan. For plainly not having done so, KTLI was fined for the violation.

This case should signal broadcasters that attempting to take advantage of that narrow awareness presumption exception to the Rule is an illusive and formidable task. The best advice is for stations cautiously not to presume awareness in any situation other than that involving a contestant calling in who is obviously familiar with the custom of the station to broadcast such calls. The safest use of this exception is the phone call-in program. To attempt it in the context of contestants calling the station to play a game is to take a legal risk.

Warnings Made Part of the Station's Permanent Record

Buffalo, New York

One "Funny Phone Call" segment aired by radio station WKBW in 1971 involved a disc jockey engaging a local housewife in a prank phone call. Claiming to represent a fictitious plumbing company, he telephoned the woman and asked if he could come to her home and take a picture of her with her new toilet. Having not purchased any new plumbing fixtures, she hung up. Yet, he called back two more times in an effort to elicit entertaining responses from the unwary victim.

Once she learned all the facts, the woman protested to the FCC. The question was whether WKBW had violated Section 73.1206 in recording the conversations but never broadcasting them.

The station's standard operating procedure relative to phone calls placed by its deejays was:

1) the conversation would be recorded from the moment the party answered—although the calls were never broadcast over the air live, simultaneously with their occurrence;

2) that taped conversation would not be broadcast without the subsequent permission of the party called once that person was apprised of the prank;

3) the announcer would disclose his identity after "the need for surprise had passed."[16]

The licensee argued that these procedures constituted internal safeguards which met the concerns which the FCC had articulated for the rights of the listeners who were called by the station; and that therefore 73.1206 had not been contravened.

Unmoved, the Commission reminded WKBW of the express language of the Rule ["Before recording a telephone conversation for broadcast,"[17] . . . the party must be notified] and determined it had been clearly violated.

As the Rule had only been adopted a year before, the Commission did not fine the station but instead noted this infraction on the broadcaster's permanent record. The significance of the decision is two-fold.

First, if a station intends to broadcast—albeit at a later time—any telephone conversation of this type, the person called must be properly notified before the call is recorded on tape.

Secondly, the only effective way to comply with any FCC Rule, this one included, is to follow the precise language of the regulation as enacted rather than develop internal station alternatives designed to accomplish what the station perceives as the purpose of the Rule. Don't be creative—be guided only by the plain language of the regulations.

Phoenix, Arizona

Similarly, the practice of Phoenix station KOY disc jockeys was to place and record prank phone calls. At the conclusion of the conversation, they would give notice and ask the parties called for their permission to subsequently broadcast the prank calls.

A 1971 incident involved one of these calls to a local business which was recorded without the party's notification or consent.

While admitting that it never had a chance to notify and seek permission of this particular victim because he hung up on the announcer in disgust, KOY assumed its typical procedure met the requirements of Rule 73.1206. With reasoning comparable to that employed in the WKBW decision, the FCC found that KOY had violated the Rule and directed that the station's permanent record be documented to reflect it.[18]

Marinette, Wisconsin

The April 1, 1971, April Fool's Day edition of a WLOT program in Marinette featured a disc jockey's call to the owner of a downtown beauty salon. The conversation was broadcast live without the businessman's knowledge.

The premise of the hoax was that the deejay angrily complained that his wife's hair had fallen out after her most recent visit and demanded to know what the startled proprietor was going to do about it.

Upon subsequently learning that the call had been broadcast, the salon owner complained to the FCC. He contended that many listeners believed the scenario, did not understand it was a joke, and that his business would seriously suffer from the report of the damage to the woman's hair.

The FCC found that not only had this broadcast obviously violated the notice and consent requirements of Rule 73.1206, but that it approached the "type of harassment"[19] and station misconduct that injures the public and is therefore intolerable. The Commission dispatched a strongly worded letter of reprimand to WLOT and made it a part of the station's permanent record for future consideration.

Rule Violation Found But No Sanction Imposed

Tucson, Arizona

The application for renewal of the license of Tucson station KIKX (see chapter 2) was designated for hearing on eleven different issues, including whether the station had violated Section 73.1206.

The allegation before the Commission was that in May of 1976, KIKX disc jockey Arthur Gopen recorded and broadcast a telephone conversation with a police department secretary without her knowledge or consent.

Earlier in that day, Gopen had phoned Tucson police officer Joseph Dotseth and sought his permission to call back a short time later while on the air and report that his (Gopen's) shoes had been stolen. It was Gopen's plan to entertain his audience with that attempt to file a missing shoe report. As the FCC investigation revealed, "Dotseth agreed to cooperate and granted permission to have the subsequent conversation recorded for later broadcast."[20]

As arranged, Gopen then placed the call with the station's tape recorders running. A secretary at the police station—one Doris Galbreath—answered the call and her brief conversation with Gopen was recorded and broadcast later along with the full conversation with Officer Dotseth.

It was undisputed that Gopen had not notified the secretary that their conversation was being recorded and the Administrative Law Judge therefore found that the Rule had been violated.

However, in part because Officer Dotseth had consented to the recording of his part of the conversation, the Judge concluded that the violation should not be punished.

Of course, in the end, the FCC revoked the station's license after considering the other ten designated issues, prominent among which was contest impropriety and the broadcast of falsehoods in the perpetration of the Gopen kidnapping hoax.[21]

Apparently, the Commission saw no point in issuing a warning to KIKX regarding the 73.1206 violation or noting such infraction in the station's permanent record, as it had done with other violators, because as a result of its revocation decision the station was forced off the air, anyway.

Declaratory Rulings and Interpretations of the Rule

Portland, Oregon

The FCC monitored KKEY's programming in August of 1971 and discovered that disc jockey Jack Hurd placed several calls to listeners during his airtime. His practice was to call a particular number, wait for the party to answer, ask the name of the person who answered, and then say either "Hello, this is Jack Hurd, KKEY on-the-air"[22] or "This is Jack Hurd, we're on the air."[23]

At this point, Hurd would engage the person in conversation on some topic of current interest. The entire conversation would typically be broadcast simultaneously, live over the air.

The FCC decided that this practice violated Section 73.1206 in two respects. First, as the notice did not alert the person called before the broadcasting of the conversation had begun, it denied that person "a real opportunity to refuse to have his conversation broadcast while not yet on the air"[24] and therefore constituted inadequate notice.

Second, the Commission faulted the language employed by the deejay as being insufficient to clearly impart to the person called the fact that the call was being broadcast. As the FCC noted, the phrase " 'Jack Hurd on-the-air' could denote the name of Mr. Hurd's program or show.''[25]

The response of the agency was to send KKEY a letter advising it that it had misinterpreted Section 73.1206 and its requirements.

This decision emphasizes the importance of using legally correct language in notifying parties who are called. The phrases set out earlier in this chapter meet the requirements of the Rule and avoid misinterpretation.

Hollywood, California

In a 1976 declaratory ruling, the FCC made it plain that Rule 73.1206 required always notifying persons called even if it prevented the surprise or entertainment value the broadcaster sought in placing the call in the first place.

The factual context involved a program concept of an independent television program producer which, in order that the show could be aired, sought a waiver of the notice requirements of the Rule. The format featured celebrities placing telephone calls to numbers chosen at random from phone books and engaging the people called in entertaining and funny conversations. Those called would not be told the call was being taped or that a studio audience was hearing all of it at the time.

The entire program would be recorded on videotape for broadcast at a later time. The producers proposed to comply with the spirit of Section 73.1206 by appropriately notifying the person called at the conclusion of the call. At that time, the consent of that party to the later broadcast of the call would be sought. If none was given, the videotape would be erased.

The producers vigorously argued that strict compliance with the advance notice requirements would destroy the spontaneity essential for the conversation to be entertaining.

The FCC denied the waiver. Analyzing the calls from the

viewers' perspective as it had attempted in past decisions to sug-
gest broadcasters do, it found that even if consent were not giv-
en and the recording not used on the air, an invasion of that
person's privacy had occurred:

> The intrusion may lead to his [the person called] embar-
> rassment or humiliation . . . before a live, studio audience
> . . . before the party called would have had an opportunity
> to refuse consent.[26]

This decision clearly subordinates the commercial programming interests of producers and broadcasters to the interest of
individuals in being protected from invasions of privacy and the
potential embarrassment or humiliation such phone calls could
cause.

The impact is that the FCC has already weighed these competing interests—the broadcasters' concerns that advance notice
will destroy spontaneity and emasculate the entertainment value
of these calls against the public's privacy and dignity interests—
and struck the balance in favor of the public.[27]

IV. EFFORTS BY BROADCASTERS TO CHANGE THE LAW

In 1983, the National Association of Broadcasters formally
petitioned the FCC to modify Rule 73.1206. Characterizing the
rule's requirement that parties called by a station be notified
before the entire phone conversation is recorded or broadcast as
"overly rigid,"[28] the NAB proposed the rule be liberalized.
Specifically, it was urged that the FCC allow the broadcast of
such conversations in their entirety if either the station identifies
itself at the outset after the person answers the phone and in-
forms him or her that "we're on the air," or, if without identifying itself at first, the station later in the conversation obtains the
explicit consent of the party to subsequently broadcast the
recorded conversation.

While the NAB's first proposal would admittedly constitute only a minor modification of the present rule, the second would make major changes and, in the NAB's view, allow broadcasters to capture on tape the spontaneity and extra spark which would be generated if the contestant called was unaware the conversation was being recorded.

The NAB predicts that the FCC will at least consider its petition in 1985 and perhaps initiate a rule-making proceeding to allow the public to offer comments on the NAB proposals.[29] So, there remains some prospect that the Commission might relax its telephone rule in the future. But for now, broadcasters must simply live with the current rule and conduct their contests the best they can utilizing the phrases for their on-air personalities suggested in this chapter.

NOTES/12

1. 47 C.F.R. § 73.1206 (1983). The Rule provides:

   Before recording a telephone conversation for broadcast, or broadcasting such a conversation simultaneously with its occurrence, a licensee shall inform any party to the call of the licensee's intention to broadcast the conversation, except where such party is aware, or may be presumed to be aware from the circumstances of the conversation, that it is being or likely will be broadcast. Such awareness is presumed to exist only when the other party to the call is associated with the station (such as an employee or part-time reporter), or where the other party originates the call and it is obvious that it is in connection with a program in which the station customarily broadcasts telephone conversations.

   See also 47 U.S.C. § 605 (1982).

2. *Broadcasting of Telephone Conversations*, 23 FCC 2d 1 (1970).

3. *Use of Recording Devices*, 11 FCC 1003 (1947); *Use of Recording Devices in Connection with Telephone*, 12 FCC 1005 (1948); *Use of Recording Devices in Connection With Telephone*, 12 FCC 1008 (1948).

4. *Use of Recording Devices*, 11 FCC 1003, 1050 (1947).

5. *Ibid.*

6. *Recording Devices*, 38 FCC 2d 579 (1972).

7. *Ibid.*

8. *Public Notice Re Contests and Promotions Which Adversely Affect the Public Interest*, 2 FCC 2d 464 (1966).

9. *Station-Initiated Telephone Calls*, 35 FCC 2d 940 (1972).

10. *Ibid.*, 941.

11. *Ibid.*, 942. See 47 U.S.C. § 223 (1982).

12. *Heftel Broadcasting-Contemporary, Inc.*, et al., 52 FCC 2d 1005 (1975). See also *Heftel Broadcasting-Contemporary, Inc.*, et al., 54 FCC 2d 1163 (1975) [Petition for remission of forfeiture denied by the Commission.]

13. 47 C.F.R. § 73.1206 (1983).

14. In a rather amusing case on point, a KBRO (Bremerton, Washington) newsman telephoned a recently announced candidate for Public Works Commissioner. According to pleadings filed with the FCC, the newsman first asked why the person was running since he knew he couldn't win. The startled candidate responded by defending his decision, and then the newsman informed him that any further comments would be recorded. In response to a complaint filed by the candidate, the FCC determined that the station had not violated Section 73.1206. *Fairness Doctrine Ruling*, 46 FCC 2d 514 (1974).

15. *Radio Beaumont, Inc.*, 47 FCC 2d 821, 822 (1974). See also *Radio Beaumont, Inc.*, 50 FCC 2d 904 (1975). [Petition for remission of forfeiture denied by the Commission.]

16. *Harassment-Telephone Call*, 35 FCC 2d 92, 93 (1972).

17. 47 C.F.R. § 73.1206 (1983).

18. *Harassment-Telephone Call*, 35 FCC 2d 90 (1972).

19. *Harassment-Telephone Call*, 35 FCC 2d 88, 89 (1972).

20. *Walton Broadcasting, Inc.*, 78 FCC 2d 880, 912 (1976). [Initial Decision of Administrative Law Judge Thomas B. Fitzpatrick].

21. *Walton Broadcasting, Inc.*, 78 FCC 2d 857 (1980).

22. *Western Broadcasting Co.*, 25 Rad. Reg. 2d 1160 (1972).

23. *Ibid.*

24. *Ibid.*, 1161.

25. *Ibid.*

26. *Quantro Productions,* 62 FCC 2d 725, 726 (1976).

27. Technically, note that the Quantro production company is not a licensee of the FCC and Section 73.1206 therefore does not apply directly to it. Too, 73.1206 reaches licensee-originated calls; and no station-initiated calls were involved here.

   But, Quantro sought the FCC Rule Waiver in this case so that licensees later carrying the show would not jeopardize their licenses or incur FCC penalties by violating Rule 73.1206.

28. National Association of Broadcasters' Petition for Rule Making, filed October 12, 1983 In the Matter of Live Broadcast of Telephone Conversations and Broadcast of Recorded Telephone Conversations, RM 4068 and 2571 before the Federal Communications Commission.

29. January 16, 1985, telephone conversation (not recorded) with Barry D. Umansky, Esquire, counsel for the National Association of Broadcasters in Washington, DC.

CHAPTER 13

Invasion of Privacy Suits by Angry Contestants

While the major legal pitfall to be avoided is broadcasting a contestant's voice contrary to the limitations of Section 73.1206 and thereby inviting a Commission fine, broadcasters should be alert to the emergence of a different legal threat: lawsuits filed by contestants who are angered that their voices have been broadcast or themselves televised as part of a contest.

Civil litigation of this type has been successfully maintained in two kinds of contest situations: the unsolicited telephone call to one's home as part of a contest and the televising of a contestant participating in a quiz show that was later found to be rigged. Each will be analyzed separately.

The Unsolicited Phone Call

Salt Lake City, Utah

In 1977, Salt Lake City television station KTVX featured a "Dialing For Dollars" program. Phone numbers of area households were randomly selected from the phone book and those people were then called during the program. They were awarded cash prizes if their home TV sets were tuned to Channel 4.

One woman who was called and given a chance to win fifty dollars became so angered by it all that she filed a lawsuit against the station.

It all started when the "Dialing For Dollars" host, with fifty dollars to give away, telephoned Jean Jeppson and asked if she had her TV set on. She shot back: "I'd rather have peace in my home than all that garbage on television, even for fifty dollars."[1]

During that brief conversation, Jeppson was unaware that the TV host had announced her name and telephone number on the air. She was also not told that the conversation itself was simultaneously being broadcast.

Jeppson complained in her suit that immediately after the broadcast, she received rude and obscene calls from people all across the state. The callers were apparently quickly responding to her biting comments about TV garbage while she was being offered fifty dollars.

As a result of that avalanche of insulting calls, her suit read, she was humiliated and put in fear for her well-being.

Jeppson argued that all of that abuse was caused by the TV station invading her privacy in the first place. She told the judge that the station could not lawfully broadcast her name and telephone number without her knowledge and consent.

After considering all of Jeppson's arguments, the trial judge dismissed the case and denied her a full trial. The judge concluded that she had abandoned her right to privacy and had actually invited calls by having her name and number listed in the telephone directory.

Undaunted, she appealed the case; and by a narrow 3–2 margin, the Utah Supreme Court reversed the trial judge and ordered the case reinstated for trial. The majority of the justices agreed state law was violated when the station broadcast the viewer's name and telephone number without her consent. Because of that, they ruled, she was entitled to a full trial on the issues.

The two dissenting justices took strong exception to the majority decision. They maintained that her case was properly thrown out of the trial court for two reasons. First, Jeppson really gave permission to anybody to call her when she had her name and number listed in the phone book. Second, it was not the program host that prompted the flurry of offensive calls, but her own stinging retort to the host's friendly offer of fifty dollars.

Back at the local courthouse afterward, KTVX and Jeppson reached an out-of-court settlement of the case whereby the station agreed to pay her a sum of between $1,000 and $1,500[2] and she agreed to drop her suit.

Despite the meager return on her claim, Jean had in fact won at the state Supreme Court when she persuaded the justices that such a phone call could constitute invasion of privacy. In the language of the courthouse, they had recognized her disturbance with KTVX's contest phone call as a legitimate "cause of action." A cause of action is something somebody can sue you for and when a state Supreme Court validates a new cause of action against a local broadcaster, that's cause for concern.

The Utah court's decision really turned on the fact that the station had broadcast the conversation with Jeppson without her knowledge or consent. They termed that "abuse of her personal identity" which involves the defendant appropriating the name and likeness of the plaintiff for its own benefit without the plaintiff's consent. The benefit to the defendant-station was envisioned as recruiting yet another contestant for its program.

In the final analysis, this individual who was so sensitive about receiving phone calls and having her name broadcast to Channel 4 viewers contributed her name to a landmark court decision which will be read and remembered for decades: (Jean) Jeppson v. United Television, Inc.

INVASION OF PRIVACY SUITS

Understand that holding broadcasters liable in tort for invasion of privacy based on unsolicited contest phone calls is a new area of the law. Plaintiffs and courts are reaching outside broadcasting to find legal arguments and apply them to the contest phone call context. And there is some law to be found which is helpful to them.

The right to privacy itself is clearly recognized as an individual's constitutional right to be left alone. Conduct of defendants which intrudes upon the seclusion of a plaintiff, subjects a plaintiff's private life to unreasonable publicity or wrongfully appropriates a plaintiff's name or likeness has been considered invasion of privacy by the courts. In hundreds of cases, defendants have paid dearly in compensatory and punitive damages assessed by judges and juries for such invasions.[3]

To win an invasion of privacy case, a plaintiff generally must prove:

1) The existence of a private matter of the plaintiff in which the public has no legitimate interest;

2) Unauthorized exposure of such matter to the public by the defendant; and

3) An injury to the plaintiff, such as mental distress,

shame or humiliation caused by the defendant's conduct.

The only major area of the law in which phone calls have been successfully civilly sued upon involves the telephone harassment of debtors by finance companies and debt collectors. While the general rule is that creditors are allowed rather wide latitude to even embarrass or annoy debtors while trying to collect from them, there are limits. In the past, some collectors have exceeded all bounds of reasonableness in trying to pressure debtors into paying.

Often, insulting and threatening telephone calls to the debtor's home, place of employment or relatives were favorite techniques of the collectors. As an ironic twist, many debtors have recovered money damages from unscrupulous collectors whose obnoxious telephone tactics offended juries.[4]

In telephone debt collection harassment cases, debtors have successfully sued in situations where:

1) the intrusion was unreasonable (defined as offensive to a person of ordinary sensitivities); or

2) the telephone intrusion was accompanied by a personal home visit or mailing; or

3) one hundred or more telephone calls were made to the plaintiff; or

4) the defendant-caller was persistent in spite of the plaintiff's rebuffs and distressed condition; or

5) the caller used vile, vicious or profane language; or

6) the calls were made late at night; or

7) the contents of the calls were communicated to a number of others.[5]

Applying the legal arguments and theories of recovery recognized in the several debt collection and telephone harassment cases to the comparatively innocent contest call is a hernial reach. Yet, that attempt is being made. To analogize 100 calls of an extremist collection agency to one random call of a friendly disc jockey or host trying to give money away seems unreasonable. So does comparing a station's harmless, good faith call in the middle of an old movie to one of a bill collector in the middle of the night.

The fear of ever being successfully sued on these bases by what would be a creative and perhaps grasping attorney should be minimized. No such suit has ever been won after a full jury trial. In my opinion, a jury would be hard pressed to equate one unsolicited, friendly midafternoon "Cash Call" or "Dialing For Dollars" call to a barrage of premeditated telephone threats and extortions at the dialing fingers of an emboldened bill collector. This is especially true given the general rule that "[o]nly the more flagrant breaches of decency and propriety . . . can be reached by the tort of invasion of privacy."[6]

It would be a closer call if the conversation is broadcast without the permission of the person called. If the call is preparatory to playing the contest on the air and merely solicits the person's consent to appear later on the air by phone, the call would likely be classified innocently. Even the most offended receiver would probably regard it as merely another call during the day which disrupts one's peace—just one more aluminum siding, bogus public opinion survey or charitable solicitation phone call to which everyone is exposed. But broadcasting one's voice during such a telephone conversation to thousands or tens of thousands of others is different. A jury might consider that a gross enough invasion of a person's privacy to warrant recovery.

What impact the Jeppson case and this discussion generally should have on the conduct of station contests should be considered by station management. Note that rights to privacy can be waived by viewers or listeners and they can do just that by sending in cards or letters from which calls are made as part of a contest. Such participation would be considered a person's consent to be called or to have his or her privacy invaded. So, there's plainly no problem with that type of contest and this type of lawsuit.

Other contests in which calls to area homes are randomly made from telephone book listings should present no problem at present if before going on the air with the call, the host or deejay first receives the permission of the one called. That was where KTVX went wrong. A good everyday rule of thumb would be to always follow the notification and consent Rule and in that way avoid opening the station up to a lawsuit for invasion of privacy.

The Contestant Who Appears and Later Sues

Brace yourselves for the results of two New York cases decided in the 1960s involving the earlier TV quiz show scandals. In each, a contestant who voluntarily appeared on a TV quiz show and who later discovered the show had been fixed, was allowed to sue the broadcaster for invasion of privacy and defamation.

These decisions carve out a rather significant exception to the general rule that when contestants voluntarily appear on a broadcast, they thereby consent to having their privacy invaded. That's because they know beforehand they will appear on camera or on the air. The exception is this: if the quiz program later turns out to have been rigged, contestants can sue for invasion of privacy on the theory that they never really consented to have their voice or picture on a rigged or fixed show.

The theory of recovery is that the contestant's consent was unknowingly given in response to a deceitful offer of the program's producers who withheld from the contestant the fact that the show was fraudulent. The argument is that had the contestant known of the true dishonest nature of the contest, he or she would never have consented to appear on it. In that way, broadcasters can be sued for invasion of privacy by contestants who were once enthusiastic and eager to appear on the air and compete for prizes.

The second cause of action which the New York courts recognized against the broadcasters in these two cases was one for defamation. Also known as libel, this type of case is generally brought by one whose reputation is wrongfully damaged by another. The contestants here contended that their reputations were besmirched by appearing on rigged quiz shows and that they had been tainted by such participation. Inherent in those arguments was the notion that the public might think they, too, had been involved in the contest wrongdoing by receiving answers before the program or had been associated with such active unlawfulness while appearing on the show. Also noted was the tidal wave of adverse national publicity which engulfed the country when it was discovered the quizzes had been fixed. The contestants who sued contended their reputations had been injured by all that publicity when coupled with the notoriety each gained locally when they first appeared on the program.

The two contestants who brought suit were Leo Goldberg,[7] who had appeared as a contestant on the "$64,000 Question" and John Holt,[8] who had competed on the "$64,000 Challenge."

While these two cases have been quietly buried for twenty years in the mountain of New York civil litigation and have not enjoyed wide exposure, it is staggering to contemplate the impact on broadcasters across the country if the legal principles recognized in them ever caught on.

It would mean quite simply that even contestants who submitted post cards to enter station telephone contests could later sue for invasion of privacy and defamation if anyone at the station in any way rigged, fixed or tampered with the contest. And we have seen dozens of cases in which, despite the owner's or general manager's plain instructions to the contrary, a deejay or other employee violated the contest integrity laws. Stations would be subjected to legal assaults on two fronts: being held accountable to the FCC for violations of the contest laws and subject to Commission penalty; and being civilly liable to angered contestants and thereby subject to a jury's award of compensatory and punitive damages.

The threat of the wider use of civil suits of this type by disgruntled contestants should be seen as further proof of how important it is to station owners and managers to exert every effort to keep their station contests clean.

1. *Jeppson v. United Television,* Inc., 580 P.2d 1087 (Utah 1978).

2. Letter of August 11, 1983, from Ray R. Christensen, Esq., Christensen, Jensen & Powell, Salt Lake City, Utah, counsel for KTVX-TV.

3. Annot., 14 A.L.R.2d 750 (1950); Annot., 87 A.L.R.3rd 145 (1978); Annot., 84 A.L.R.3rd 1159 (1978); Annot., 23 A.L.R.3rd 865 (1969); and Annot., 87 A.L.R.3rd 1279 (1978).

4. Annot. 56 A.L.R.3rd 457 (1974).

5. *Ibid.*

6. *Ibid.,* 468.

7. *Goldberg v. Columbia Broadcasting System,* Inc., 205 N.Y.S.2d 611 (1960).

8. *Holt v. Columbia Broadcasting System,* Inc., 253 N.Y.S.2d 1020 (1964).

CHAPTER 14

Personal Injury Suits by the Public

Radio and television stations should also be on notice that they can be civilly sued by members of the public for any personal injuries caused by their contests. In 1975, a Los Angeles jury's $300,000 verdict against local station KHJ in just such a case was affirmed by the California Supreme Court.

Weirum v. RKO General, Inc.

In 1970, KHJ dominated the Los Angeles teen-age market with a forty-eight per cent share of those listeners. That summer, it launched a heavily promoted "Super Summer Spectacular Contest" in which disc jockey Donald Steele Revert ("the real Don Steele") drove a bright red station promotional car throughout the metropolitan area. The station would regularly broadcast his location and future destinations. The first listener to locate Steele and answer a certain question or have with them a certain article of clothing, would win a cash prize.

Seventeen-year-old Robert Sentner and nineteen-year-old Marsha Baime attempted to catch Steele on July 16. They raced against each other, their cars jockeying for position closest to Steele's car, at speeds up to eighty miles per hour on a local freeway. When Steele left the freeway, so did the two teen-agers and tragedy struck. The car of one of the teens went out of control and caused the death of one Weirum by forcing Weirum's car off the road. The victim's wife and children sued not only the two teen-age drivers but KHJ as well.

Young Sentner settled with the Weirums out of court. The case against the other youth and the station went on to trial and a jury returned a verdict of $300,000 against the defendants. The young girl did not appeal, but the station fought it out alone at the state Supreme Court. That Court later affirmed the jury's verdict in a unanimous opinion.

The pivotal question as the Court saw it was whether KHJ "owned a duty to decedent [Weirum] arising out of its broadcast of the giveaway contest."[1] The Justices decided that because of the risk of injury that was attendant to this particular contest, the station in fact owed a duty of due care to the public in general and to Weirum in particular. For breaching that duty to insure the safety and health of its listeners and the public, KHJ was found civilly liable for the injuries and wrongful death of Mr. Weirum.

In its defense, the station vigorously protested that it had no control over the real cause of Weirum's death—the teen-ager's car which spun out of control and precipitated Weirum's crash. The jury and Supreme Court disagreed. Said the court:

> It was foreseeable that defendant's youthful listeners, find-
> ing the prize had eluded them at one location, would race
> to arrive first at the next site and in their haste would disre-
> gard the demands of highway safety.[2]

The court went on to explain that it was the dangerousness of
the contest which left the broadcaster liable:

> We need not belabor the grave danger inherent in the con-
> test broadcast by defendant . . . Defendant could have ac-
> complished its objectives of entertaining its listeners and
> increasing advertising revenues by adopting a contest for-
> mat which would have avoided danger to the motoring
> public.[3]

At bottom, then, KHJ's liability rested on foreseeability and
the dangerousness of the contest.

Injuries Which are Foreseeable

Because KHJ should have foreseen that its "Super Summer
Spectacular Contest" would have caused highway carelessness
and thereby injuries to others, it was held accountable at law.

The lynchpin for liability is reasonable foreseeability or
whether a reasonably cautious station owner or manager would
have foreseen that personal injuries or even property damage
would result from a certain contest.

Broadcasters must be sensitive to this legal danger and revise
their contest planning and development check-list accordingly.
When any contest is considered, one black letter agenda item at
the staff or management meeting that is called to approve such
contest must be "injuries foreseeable." Input should be solicited
from several on the management team and on the staff; prudence
and caution should be the marching orders. All should be asked
to brainstorm and predict likely personal injuries or property
damage that could be caused by the contest or its contestants. If
the final decision-maker(s) then develop a reasonable concern

that injuries or damages could possibly result from the proposed contest, it should be scrapped.

Dangerous Contests

Those types of contests which involve an inherent risk of serious injury to the public should never be aired. That's because of the inherent legal risk that the station could be successfully sued for those injuries, as KHJ was.

Broadcasters considering specific contests which are proposed to them should categorize each contest idea as either dangerous or not, and then reject the dangerous ones summarily.

There are two kinds of injuries to which stations must be alert. The first, property damage, could quite predictably result from treasure hunt contestants trampling homeowners' lawns, gardens and shrubs hysterically searching for some hidden clue or prize. Under the California Supreme Court's reasoning in *Weirum,* any owners of private property so damaged could successfully sue the station which conducted the treasure hunt.

Due to the fact that risk of property damage is inherent in treasure hunt contests, they should either be avoided entirely or planned conservatively. The only safe treasure hunt in terms of insulating the station from lawsuits would be one which is conducted exclusively on public property. And that limitation should be emphatically emphasized to the treasure hunters in no uncertain terms during contest promos. If a station is intent on hiding buried treasure, it should be done in a public park, a playground, a beach or other appropriate safe public area.

The second kind of injury for which stations can be sued is personal, physical harm to a member of the public. That's what happened in *Weirum,* of course. Spurred to carelessness by the station's contest, contestants injured a member of the public. And the California Supreme Court saved some of its harshest language for a condemnation of KHJ's decision to air such a dangerous contest.

The bottom line is that if any proposed contest would pose a danger to the public, it should never reach the air. Common sense would classify contests involving automobiles and high speed chases as inherently dangerous to the public. If a station car travelling on the streets is part of the contest script, a red flag should flutter in the broadcaster's mind. The dangers to other motorists, bystanders and pedestrians are obvious.

Yet, contests using station cars are still broadcast. In November of 1982, KFI listeners in Southern California were given the chance to win a new Chevy Chevette. Participating California Chevrolet dealers first distributed free "I Want A Chevette" bumper stickers to contestants. Then KFI "Cash Cars" were dispatched to search for cars bearing the Chevette bumper stickers. Contestants listening to KFI were given clues throughout each day as to the location of the travelling "Cash Cars."

Whenever the driver of one of the KFI cars saw one of the bumper stickers, he would signal the car over to the side of the road or another place. There, the contestant was given his or her choice of several envelopes. Many envelopes contained cash; in others, a key to a new Chevette could be found.[4]

In my considered opinion, KFI took a real chance with that contest. First, contests involving moving cars on public streets are always questionable. Second, this particular contest required at least two acts on the part of participating contestant-motorists which clearly posed a danger of personal injury to other motorists. The frantic broadcasting of clues as to the whereabouts of the "Cash Cars" and the vigilance which was required of contestants in always looking for those station cars could easily have diverted their attention from the road and constituted a violation of their legal duty to maintain a proper lookout while driving. Such a contestant might have rammed another car or clipped a pedestrian in a cross-walk with his or her attention diverted from the business of driving to the fun of tracking a "Cash Car." And the very act of pulling a contestant's car over in lanes of traffic to play the envelope game clearly posed a danger to other motorists on the streets. Highway patrolmen pull cars over to the side of the road. Radio station fleets have no legitimate business doing so. Had another motorist or pedestrian been injured in either of these ways, KFI would have been wide open to a lawsuit.

In determining which contests generally pose dangers of personal injury to the public, the focus should be on the instrumentalities of the contest. Moving cars are dangerous and contests involving them therefore create risks. Similarly, motorcycles, mopeds and snowmobiles are dangerous instrumentalities and should not be part of a contest's scenario. Also on the dangerous list are animals such as horses and stray dogs; and places such as power lines, generating plants and city streets.

Dangerous Promotions

Broadcasters should be alerted to a new development in the law which has emerged not from contests, but from station-sponsored promotions.

The problem promotion involves a radio station, typically, hosting a party or happy hour for its listeners and the general public at a local bar, pub or beer garden. Of course, alcoholic beverages are either sold or provided free at these parties.

The potential for liability is that those stations can be sued if someone in attendance becomes intoxicated and injures another motorist or pedestrian on his or her way home. The victim could sue the station for personal injury or wrongful death on a "dram shop" type theory of recovery—that is, that the station in part caused the injury or death by providing beer or liquor to an individual who had become obviously intoxicated and who then left the station's party and drove drunk, causing an injury.

And the survivors of a victim of a drunk driver successfully argued essentially that in a recent Kansas City case. There, a 19-year old, who was changing a tire on the highway, was killed by a drunk driver who ran into him. In addition to the bar that served the driver too much beer, the victim's parents sued the Kansas City area radio station which had aired several ads for free beer which had attracted the driver to the bar in the first place.

The parents claimed that the station was at least partially at fault in contributing to the driver's drunkenness. That suit against the broadcaster was settled out of court with the payment by the station of an undisclosed amount to the parents. The insurance company representing the defendant driver paid the parents $20,000.[5]

Clearing Those Contests

It is incumbent on the broadcaster to be sensitive to the dangers that certain types of contests and particular contest instrumentalities represent. Each proposed contest should then be categorized on that basis, as either potentially dangerous or not when the station makes an honest assessment of contest ideas as part of its heightened first alert scrutiny of all contests. During that process, of course, the specific question of whether any injuries are foreseeable must also be asked.

The intelligent broadcaster will carefully think through each and every contest idea with these legal pitfalls in mind as part of a contest clearance checklist.[6] And simply put, contests which create an unreasonable risk of personal injury or property damage to the public should not be aired. That is the lesson of *Weirum* remembered.

NOTES/14

1. *Weirum v. RKO General, Inc.*, 539 P.2d 36, 39 (Calif. 1975).

2. *Ibid.*, 40.

3. *Ibid.*

4. *Broadcasters Promotion Association, Inc., Newsletter,* March, 1983, at 10.

5. Telephone interview with Craig J. Blakely, Esquire, of the Washington, D.C. law firm of Schnader, Harrison, Segal & Lewis on Jan. 16, 1985. See also "Questions Left Unanswered in Kansas City," *Broadcasting,* Sept. 24, 1984.

6. See Chapter 17 for a complete contest checklist.

CHAPTER 15

Bookkeeping and I.R.S. Details

Painstaking and competent accounting, billing and record keeping are vital to the operation of any well run station. Contest bookkeeping is particularly important because of the special legal liability and tax issues involved. Yet, with the forms and guidance provided in this chapter, a station's on-staff bookkeeper or secretary will be able to fully comply with the law and keep exactly those records which the station's accountant or tax attorney will need at tax time.

Any station's contest bookkeeping machinery can be automatic, mechanical and smooth running. It definitely need not be time consuming or burdensome. It can be painlessly done in-house and correctly from contest conception to the time the tax forms are filed.

The Bookkeeper's Role in any Station Contest

First Responsibility

A separate file or ledger page must be maintained for each contest.

Second Responsibility

The station can deduct, as reasonable business expenses, the necessary and ordinary costs of conducting any of its own contests.[1] These costs will include the money spent for newspaper advertising, billboards, printing, any other advertising or promotion, travel, production and the purchase of prizes. Because of the deductibility of all of these expenses, the bookkeeper must record and document each.

Third Responsibility

Records must be kept of any money received from businesses participating in the contest as that will be included as station income for tax purposes.[2]

Fourth Responsibility

As soon as any contest winner is named, an affidavit should be mailed to that individual. A complete contest affidavit form is provided on page 170. The document first congratulates the winner, and then asks that he or she certify that all contest eligibility requirements were met, that no federal contest integrity laws were violated and that he or she did not receive any secret or special assistance from the station. The form also contains two clauses which provide legal protection for the station—a forfeiture provision and one releasing the station from all liability in connection with the prize. Lastly, a release is included which permits the station to use the winner's name, voice and photograph in its advertising.

No prize should be awarded until the affidavit is completed and returned by the winner.

Fifth Responsibility

At the time that the station awards the prize, the winner must be furnished with a contest prize receipt prepared for his or her signature.

In this important document, which appears on page 000, the winner acknowledges receipt of the prize and the satisfaction of all station obligations, accepts responsibility for paying the tax on any prize worth $600 or more and notes the obligation of the station to notify the I.R.S. of the winner's name when any prize valued at $600 or more is awarded. The prizewinner is asked to provide his or her Social Security number and complete home address so that the station can effortlessly complete the necessary I.R.S. forms.

Before submission to the prizewinner, several blanks on the contest prize receipt form need be completed by the station's bookkeeper. Information to be provided includes the date on which the prize was won, the name of the contest, a description of the prize and the value of the prize.

The value of the prize is key because if it is $600 or more, the winner must pay taxes on it and the station must submit certain forms to the I.R.S.[3] If the value is less than $600, there are no such requirements and the bookkeeper can take the afternoon off.

There are four perfectly acceptable methods for computing the value of a contest prize. First, if the prize won was cash, the value is obviously exactly the amount that was awarded. Second, if the station purchases a prize full price at retail and pays $250 for it, that's the value. Third, if the station is given a substantial price break by a retailer in exchange for some ad time or for any other reason, the value of the prize will be the manufacturer's suggested retail selling price of the item or its fair market value. The station can choose which one. Fourth, if a business provides an item free in return for a certain number of spots, the value of that item to be reported on this form and later to the I.R.S. (if $600 or over) will be the station's choice of either the manufacturer's suggested retail selling price or the fair market value of the item.[4]

The method by which the station makes its computation is to be noted on the form.

Logistically, there are two ways to effect the distribution of the prize and the completion of the contest prize receipt.

The better approach is to ask the winner to personally come down to the station to pick up the prize; and at that time to hand him or her the receipt form and actually see to it that it is correctly signed. This would be especially necessary if the value of the prize is $600 or more.

The second approach is to mail the prize to the winner and include the receipt, together with a note requesting that it be completed and returned immediately. This method would be acceptable in those instances when the value of the prize is less than $600.

Sixth Responsibility

Throughout the year, a list must be religiously maintained of those contestants who win prizes valued at $600 or more. It is necessary that such list include the names, complete residence addresses and Social Security numbers of those prizewinners.

In January of each new year, a station's bookkeeper simply uses the prizewinner list of the previous twelve months (the tax year) to comply with the federal tax laws. This can be done in two ways. First, the bookkeeper can merely provide the station's tax attorney or accountant with the list so that the proper I.R.S. forms can be completed. Or second, the bookkeeper can quickly handle all I.R.S. paperwork alone by typing the name and address of the station, the name, address and Social Security number of the prizewinner and the value of the prize on a short I.R.S. Form 1099-MISC. Required by law to be completed in triplicate, one copy of each 1099 is to be included with the station's tax return to the I.R.S., one copy is to be sent to the prizewinner and one copy is to be retained by the station for its records. The prizewinner's copy must be mailed to him or her by January 31.[5]

One simple 1099 form is to be filled out for each contestant who has won a prize worth $600 or more during the tax year. The copies of those 1099s scheduled to be sent to the I.R.S. are then attached to an I.R.S. Form 1096, which is a summary sheet on which the station indicates the total of 1099s being filed and the broadcaster's federal identifying number. Completed sample 1099 and 1096 forms appear on pages 173–176.

The only other contest tax responsibilities for the bookkeeper will be to report any money generated by the contest as income to the station and list the contest's costs as deductible business expenses.

SAMPLE AFFIDAVIT

WXYZ RADIO

TO: All Prize Winners   FROM: WXYZ Radio

Congratulations on being selected as a WXYZ contest prize winner. To satisfy certain legal points, we ask that all winners read, complete and sign the following form. Please do so and return this page to: Promotion Department, WXYZ Radio, Box 1320, Anytown, USA 50311. Your prize will be awarded to you when we receive this form.

Thank you.

Mr. Local Broadcaster, President
WXYZ Radio

WXYZ RADIO — CONTEST AFFIDAVIT

1. I hereby certify that I meet all of the eligibility requirements as stated in the terms of the contest.

2. I certify that I did not violate any of the federal laws prohibiting contest impropriety, that I did not receive any special or secret aid or assistance, and that I did not participate in any scheme to rig, fix or predetermine the outcome of the contest I won.

3. I certify that I am the person who won the contest and that my true name, address, age and Social Security number are listed below.

4. I understand that WXYZ Radio has the right to request that I appear in person at their studios/offices to pick up my prize.

5. I understand that I may be required to forfeit any prize won if any representations made by me herein are not true.

6. I hereby release and discharge WXYZ Broadcasting Corp., WXYZ Radio, and its officers and employeees from any liability for any injuries or damages or causes of action arising out of or in connection with said contest or attendant to my acceptance and use of the prize won.

_____   _____
(Prize Winner's Signature)   (Prize Winner's Social Security Number)

_____   _____
(Please Print Full name)   (Prize Winner's birthdate)

_____   _____
(Prize Winner's complete address)   (Today's date)

_____
(Parent/Guardian signature if winner is under 18 years of age)

7. OPTIONAL: I will _____; or I will not _____ (check one) permit WXYZ to use my name, photograph, likeness, video or audio recordings of my voice and brief biographical summary for advertising and publicizing WXYZ and its contests in connection with the prize I won. I understand that I am not required to agree to this use in order to receive the prize I won.

PLEASE COMPLETE AND SIGN THIS FORM AT ONCE AND RETURN IT TO WXYZ RADIO, BOX 1320, ANYTOWN, U.S.A. 50311. PRIZES ARE GENERALLY RELEASED TO WINNERS WITHIN 30 DAYS OF THE DATE ON WHICH THE PRIZE WAS WON.

170

SAMPLE PRIZE RECEIPT
WXYZ RADIO

TO: All Prize Winners   FROM: WXYZ Radio

To satisfy certain requirements imposed by law, this form is to be completed and signed by you at the time the prize you won is awarded to you.

Once again, congratulations and thank you for listening to WXYZ Radio. We hope you thoroughly enjoy your prize.

Mr. Local Broadcaster, President
WXYZ Radio

WXYZ RADIO — CONTEST PRIZE RECEIPT

1. I received today from the WXYZ Broadcasting Corp. and WXYZ Radio the contest prize described below. I won the prize in the contest listed below.

2. I acknowledge that the WXYZ Broadcasting Corp. and WXYZ Radio have totally fulfilled their obligations to me as a prizewinner in this contest. I hold no further claims on WXYZ.

3. I understand that if the value of my prize is $600 or more, it is my duty to declare that amount as income and pay the applicable federal and state income taxes. I also understand that WXYZ Radio is required by law to report the award of any prize worth $600 or more to the Internal Revenue Service. The law also requires WXYZ to send me a copy of the I.R.S. Form 1099 upon which they report my prize to the I.R.S.

THE FOLLOWING TO BE COMPLETED BY WXYZ:

A. DATE ON WHICH PRIZE WAS WON _____

B. NAME OF CONTEST_____

C. THE PRIZE WON (DESCRIPTION) _____
_____

D. IDENTIFICATION OF SERIAL NUMBER OF PRIZE,
IF APPLICABLE _____

E. VALUE OF THE PRIZE _____

   -COMPUTED ON: Manufacturer's Suggested Retail Price   (_____); or

   (CHECK ONE)   Fair Market Value   (_____); or

                        The prize was cash   (_____).

THE FOLLOWING TO BE COMPLETED BY THE PRIZEWINNER:

A. TODAY'S DATE_____

B. PRIZEWINNER'S SIGNATURE _____

C. PRIZEWINNER'S NAME, PRINTED _____

D. PRIZEWINNER'S COMPLETE HOME ADDRESS _____
(STREET, CITY, ZIP CODE) _____

E. PRIZEWINNER'S SOCIAL SECURITY NUMBER _____

PLEASE MAIL THIS COMPLETED AND SIGNED FORM IMMEDIATELY TO: WXYZ Radio, P.O. Box 1320, Anytown, U.S.A. 50311.

SAMPLE PROMOTIONAL EVENT RELEASE FORM

(To be used in those station-sponsored events requiring pre-registration or on-site registration of participants, including events co-sponsored by the station.)

I wish to participate in (insert name of promotional event) on (insert date), an event sponsored (or co-sponsored) by WXYZ Radio.

In consideration for WXYZ Radio permitting me to participate in the said (insert name of event), I hereby agree to release and discharge WXYZ Broadcasting Corp., WXYZ Radio, and its officers and employees from any liability for any injuries or damages or causes of action arising out of or in connection with said event.

In consideration for WXYZ Radio permitting me to participate in the said (insert name of event), I hereby grant WXYZ permission to use my name, photograph, likeness, video and/or audio recordings of my person and voice and biographical material for advertising and publicizing WXYZ and said event.

_____   _____
(Participant's Signature)   (Today's Date)

_____   _____
(Please Print Full Name)   (Parent/Guardian Signature if
                                     Participant is under 18 years of age)

_____
(Participant's Complete Address)

6969

For Official Use Only

1096

Department of the Treasury
Internal Revenue Service

Annual Summary and Transmittal of U.S. Information Returns

OMB No. 1545-0108

19**84**

or machine print PAYER'S name

XYZ Broadcasting Corp.

t address

320 Cash Call Way

State and ZIP code

nytown, U.S.A.

Enter in Box 1 or 2 below the identifying number you used as the payer on the attached information returns. Do not fill in both Boxes 1 and 2.

1 Employer identification number	2 Social security number
INSERT YOUR NUMBER	NOT the payee's SSN
3 Total number of documents	4 Number without taxpayer ID numbers
one	none

	Regular 1099's and 5498's								Nominee/Middleman 1099's							
	1099 B 79	1099 DIV 91	1099 G 86	1099 INT 92	1099 MISC 95	1099 OID 96	1099 PATR 97	5498 28	1099 ASC 84	1099 B 79	1099 DIV 91	1099 G 86	1099 INT 92	1099 MISC 95	1099 OID 96	1099 PATR 97
☐	☐	☐	☐	☐	☐	☐	☐	☐	☐	☐	☐	☐	☐	☒	☐	☐

der penalties of perjury, I declare that I have examined this return, including accompanying documents and to the best of my knowledge and belief, they are true, correct, omplete. In the case of documents without recipients' identifying numbers I have complied with the requirements of the law in attempting to secure such numbers from cipients.

ture ▶ *Mr. Local Broadcaster*   Title ▶ *President*   Date ▶ *4-1-85*

Please return this entire page to the Internal Revenue Service.

rwork Reduction Act Notice

k for this information to carry out the Internal Revenue f the United States. We need it to ensure that taxpayers mplying with these laws and to allow us to figure and : the right amount of tax. You are required to give us this ation.

ce to Payers

ose of this Form.—Use this form to transmit Forms and 5498 to the Internal Revenue Service. However, orm W-3G to transmit Form 1099-R.

er your name, address, and taxpayer identifying er (TIN) in the spaces provided on the form. Individuals a trade or business should enter their social security er in box 2; sole proprietors and all others should enter employer identification number in box 1. However, sole ietors who are not required to have an employer fication number should enter their social security er in box 2.

not submit more than one type of Form 1099 or submit 5498 and Forms 1099 with the same Form 1096.

In box 3, enter the number of documents attached to Form 1096 and check the appropriate box to indicate the type of Form 1099 (or 5498) you are transmitting.

If you are transmitting Forms 1099 as a nominee or middleman for payments you received on behalf of another person, check the appropriate box on the lower right half of this form. If you are required to file both regular Forms 1099 or 5498 and Forms 1099 as a middleman or nominee, use a separate Form 1096 for each category.

If you have one type of Form 1099 (or 5498) that includes forms with TIN's of recipients and others with no TIN's, you may submit them with one Form 1096 if they are bundled separately. Show the total number of documents being transmitted in box 3. Also, show the number of forms without TIN's in box 4.

For more information about where and when to file, etc., see the separate instructions for Form 1096.

If you are filing a Form 1096 for corrected information returns mark over the "X" in the box at the top left corner of this form.

☆ U.S.G.P.O.   1984: 423-326   36-2249473

173

174

1984

Statement for
Recipients of
**Miscellaneous
Income**

For Paperwork
Reduction Act Notice
and instructions for
completing this form,
see Instructions for
Form 1096.

**Copy A
For Internal Revenue
Service Center**

☒ **9595** ☐ VOID		
Type or machine print PAYER'S name **WXYZ Broadcasting Corp.**	1 Rents	2 Royalties
Street address **1320 Cash Call Way**	3 Prizes and awards **$600.00**	4 Federal income tax withheld
City, State, and ZIP code **Anytown, U.S.A.**	5 Fishing boat proceeds	6 Medical and health care payments
Federal identifying number **Insert federal ID number**	Recipient's identifying number **SSN 479-00-0000**	7 Nonemployee compensation
Type or machine print RECIPIENT'S name (first, middle, last) **Daniel L. Power**	8 Payer made direct sales of $5,000 or more of consumer products to a buyer (recipient) for resale. . . . . ▶ ☐	
Street address **2700 Carpenter Street**		
City, State, and ZIP code **Des Moines, Iowa 50311**		

Form **1099-MISC**

Department of the Treasury - Internal Revenue Service

PAYER'S name, address, ZIP code, and Federal identifying number.

WXYZ Broadcasting Corp.
1320 Cash Call Way
Anytown, U.S.A.
PLUS FEDERAL IDENTIFYING NUMBER

RECIPIENT'S name, address, and ZIP code.

Daniel L. Power
2700 Carpenter Street
Des Moines, Iowa 50311

	1 Rents	2 Royalties
	3 Prizes and awards $600.00	4 Federal income tax withheld
	5 Fishing boat proceeds	6 Medical and health care payments
Recipient's identifying number SSN 479-00-0000		7 Nonemployee compensation
8 Payer made direct sales of $5,000 or more of consumer products to a buyer (recipient) for resale. .... ▲ ☐		

OMB No.1545-0115

1984

Statement for
Recipients of
**Miscellaneous
Income**

For Paperwork
Reduction Act Notice
and instructions for
completing this form,
see Instructions for
Form 1096.

**Copy C
For Payer**

Form **1099-MISC**

Department of the Treasury - Internal Revenue Service

175

PAYER'S name, address, ZIP code, and Federal identifying number.

WXYZ Broadcasting Corp.
1320 Cash Call Way
Anytown, U.S.A.
PLUS FEDERAL IDENTIFYING NUMBER

RECIPIENT'S name, address, and ZIP code.

Daniel L. Power
2700 Carpenter Street
Des Moines, Iowa 50311

Form **1099-MISC**

1 Rents	**2** Royalties
3 Prizes and awards $600.00	**4** Federal income tax withheld
5 Fishing boat proceeds	**6** Medical and health care payments
Recipient's identifying number SSN 479-00-0000	**7** Nonemployee compensation
8 Payer made direct sales of $5,000 or more of consumer products to a buyer (recipient) for resale. . . . . ▶ ☐	

OMB No. 1545-0115

1984

Statement for
Recipients of
**Miscellaneous
Income**

**This information is
being furnished to
the Internal Revenue
Service.**

**Copy B
For Recipient**

Department of the Treasury - Internal Revenue Service

NOTES/15

1. I.R.C. § 162.

2. I.R.C. § 61.

3. Treas. Reg. § 1.6041-1 (1982).

4. Rev. Rul. 58-347, 1958-2 C.B. 878.

5. I.R.C. § 6041.

CHAPTER 16

The Lottery Laws: Liability in Contest Cases

Up until this point, this book has detailed and discussed the legal land mines which a broadcaster must avoid while airing station contests and promotions. In this chapter, the focus shifts to what are primarily contests and sales promotions conducted by local businesses. The station's involvement is usually limited to carrying spots which advertise the sponsor's games and giveaways. And there are plenty of them to advertise.

Contests and sweepstakes are highly regarded by businesses as effective techniques to stimulate sales. They bring in customers. The fact is that most Americans are continuously exposed to retailers' or manufacturers' contests or sales promotion schemes. And most people respond enthusiastically to the chance to register for a prize while they gas up or play quick Bingo for cash at the grocers.

The problem for broadcasters is that many of those sales promotions are technically "lotteries" within the strict meaning of the law. And it's a federal crime for any radio or television station to 1) air a lottery; or 2) carry an advertisement for a lottery; or 3) broadcast even any information whatever about a lottery.[1] (Exceptions for official state lotteries will be discussed later.) This federal lottery law, Section 1304 of Title 18 of the United States Code, provides for maximum penalties of a $1,-000 fine and/or one year in prison for each day the illegal lottery advertising airs.

The FCC's own lottery regulation, Section 73.1211 of its Rules, prohibits broadcast stations from carrying "any advertisement of or information concerning any lottery."[2] Infractions of this FCC rule are punishable by the full range of Commission administrative sanctions including fines, short-term renewals, license revocations, and censure or admonition.

In practice, nearly all stations which have violated the federal lottery statute and the FCC lottery rule have been proceeded against at the FCC rather than in federal court and have received either fines or license revocations. No prison sentences have been imposed.

For years, broadcasters have regarded the lottery laws as among the most confusing and complex restraints imposed on them. Many simply do not understand what is required of them by the laws, how to recognize a retailer's promotion as a lottery or how to guard against making an innocent, yet costly, lottery mistake. At the base of the problem is the difficulty most of us have in classifying the innocent grand prize drawing of a local dry cleaners as an illegal lottery. It just makes no sense.

To many, lotteries include the numbers games or the gambling associated with organized crime, not a clothing store's

game which gives customers the chance to win a trip to Nash-
ville or $5.00 off the price of a pair of designer jeans. But
legally a lottery is any scheme whereby money or prizes can be
won by chance by people who have paid valuable consideration
for that chance to win. These contests are often known by other
names—raffles, sales promotions, commercial-promotional lotteries, gift enterprises, games of chance and sweepstakes.

The U.S. Supreme Court has held that three elements must be
present in any such scheme for it to be classified as a lottery—
prize (anything of value offered to a contestant); chance (where
the winner is selected on the basis of luck or chance, rather than
skill or knowledge); and consideration (anything of value which
must be furnished by the contestant in order to participate).

Even with the Supreme Court's help, a clear working definition of an illegal lottery is difficult for many traffic managers
and ad salesmen to visualize; and several stations have paid the
price for Section 1304 violations. While most station infractions
have involved airing spots for sponsors' sales promotions which
the government later decided were lotteries, broadcasters have
also been penalized for airing PSA's for charitable raffles which
the FCC classified as lotteries and for broadcasting programs on
their own which turned out to be lotteries. To bring all of this
into sharper focus, several key FCC lottery decisions will be
analyzed.

BUSINESS SALES PROMOTIONS

Greensboro, North Carolina

The local Chrysler-Plymouth dealer set up a huge tree inside
its showroom in 1973 and unveiled a big-stakes sales promotion,
the "Money Tree." The tree was decorated with numerous envelopes, each containing a prize. The envelopes bulged with
varying amounts of cash (from five to five hundred dollars),

coupons for television sets and all expense paid vacations. The idea of the promotion was simple: any customer who purchased a new car could pluck an envelope off the glittering Money Tree.

The Chrysler dealer's ad agency bought time on television station WFMY-TV and aired a Money Tree ad sixteen times before the station discovered it was violating the lottery laws and quickly pulled the commercial. The station attempted to avoid liability by explaining it had been assured by the local attorney for the Chrysler dealer that the ad was legal. Then, it maintained the ads had been aired when its management personnel were absent from the station. The licensee also placed into evidence its exemplary broadcasting record—in the twenty-five years it had been on the air, it had always religiously followed the FCC Rules and had never received even as much as a reprimand or nominal fine for any rule violation whatever.

The Commission wasn't impressed. First, it determined that the car dealer's Money Tree gimmick was a lottery because it involved the three definitional lottery elements: prize (from cash to vacations); chance (awarded on the basis of a lucky choice of envelopes); and consideration (only purchasers of cars could take an envelope from the tree).

Then, the FCC disposed of the station's defenses in rapid-fire order. It ruled that reliance on incorrect legal advice was never a defense; that since stations are always responsible for the wrongful acts of their employees, the absence of the management on the day in question was irrelevant; and that the spotless twenty-five year broadcast record did not relieve the station of liability for this major mistake in its twenty-sixth.

WFMY-TV was ordered to pay a $5,000 fine for violating Section 1304.[3] The radio stations in the area which also carried the Money Tree ads were fined $2,000 each in separate decisions.[4]

Washington, D.C.

The Pants Ranch, a local clothier boasting 40,000 pairs of trousers in its inventory, developed a new sales scheme in 1975 to attract more customers. The store installed a wheel of fortune which could be spun by anyone buying a pair of pants. Stops on the wheel included various dollar amounts—from $2 to $10—and the amount which was spun by the customer would then be deducted from the price of the purchase.

To advertise its wheel of fortune, the Pants Ranch purchased ad time on six area radio stations owned by Metromedia, Inc.—WASH-FM, WEAM, WEEL, WHFS-FM, WMAL-FM and WPGC-FM.

When those announcements aired right in the backyard of the FCC's headquarters in the nation's capital, the Commission was quick to act. Evidence was obtained which established the Pants Ranch wheel of fortune was in fact a lottery in the eyes of the law: there was a prize offered (a discount); chance determined the winner (clearly luck in the spinning and stopping of the wheel); and consideration was required (in order to spin the wheel for a price discount, the customer had to buy the pants).

The stations protested that they didn't realize the wheel of fortune operation was a lottery. Therefore, it was argued they could not be found in violation of Section 1304 because that statute required the government to prove they "knowingly" broadcast lottery information.

The FCC interpreted the word "knowingly" to mean only that the broadcaster deliberately or knowingly aired the particular commercial, not that he know that the ad represented a lottery. Determining that information concerning a lottery had indeed thus been broadcast, the Commission fined each of the six stations from $2,000 to $3,000 for violating Section 1304 of Title 18 of the U.S. Code.[5]

St. Thomas, Virgin Islands

In 1972, J & B Scotch unveiled a sales campaign in all the liquor stores in the Virgin Islands. With each purchase of a bottle of J & B, a customer could complete an entry form by listing his or her name and address. A few weeks later, a drawing would be held and the winner awarded an elegant Rolls Royce automobile.

The advertising agency representing J & B purchased time on most Island radio stations. Five-second spots aired on WSTA in St. Thomas which encouraged listeners to visit their favorite liquor store for complete details and information on how to register for the Rolls.

An FCC investigation later revealed that the sales campaign was a lottery because it featured a prize (the car); revolved on chance (the luck of drawing one card out of thousands in the barrel); and required consideration (the purchase of a bottle of J & B before entering).

WSTA defended itself by insisting the ad agency which placed the spots never revealed that a purchase was necessary in order to enter the contest.

Apparently reasoning that it was the duty of the broadcaster to satisfy itself that the sales promotion was not being operated as a lottery rather than blindly accept the assurance of an ad agency, the FCC ruled that ignorance of the true facts of the contest was no excuse. It fined WSTA $1,000 for violating the federal lottery laws.[6]

Gainesville, Florida

The local Ford dealer launched a sales campaign in 1973 by purchasing a series of sixty-two spots on station WDVH. The ads announced that every purchaser of a new car or truck would win either a $25, $50 or $500 U.S. Savings bond. The bonds, in those varying denominations, had been randomly placed in each of the vehicles' glove boxes.

The FCC charged that WDVH had broadcast an announcement for what was in reality an illegal lottery.

The station was stunned and said it had done its level best to stay within the law in that complex lottery field. Specifically, DVH reported that it had been assured by the retailer and the ad agency that placed the spot that no lottery was involved; that it had carefully adopted station policies and guidelines to prevent the broadcast of lotteries; that it had purposely studied and learned all it could about lotteries by subscribing to trade publications, reading the FCC's Rules and Regulations and retaining Washington, D.C., communications counsel; and that it absolutely did not intend to violate the lottery law in any way.

The FCC first decided that the sales promotion was indeed a lottery as the three lottery elements were present: prize (a savings bond); chance (whether a customer won a $25 or $500 bond depended solely on luck); and consideration (in order to win, it was necessary for one to purchase a car or truck).

The Commission then found the station's arguments in its defense unpersuasive. It concluded simply that none of the circumstances and precautions reported by WDVH could deny the fact that the station broadcast an announcement for a lottery, thus violating the law. WDVH was ordered to pay a forfeiture in the amount of $2,000.[7]

Wilkes-Barre, Pennsylvania

The 1967 "Win Cash" sales promotion of Vaughn's Sanitary Bakery provided customers the opportunity to win cash right in their supermarkets. At the bakery, coupons were randomly inserted in numerous loaves of Vaughn's White Bread which could be redeemed for cash in various amounts up to twenty-five dollars. In addition to stuffing bread packages with coupons, Vaughn's also supplied grocers with quantities of free, loose coupons for those shoppers who wanted to enter the contest but didn't want to purchase the bread.

Vaughn's ad agency then bought time on area radio and television stations for spots which heralded the bread-to-riches campaign. WBRE-TV, the respondent charged here, was one of those stations. The ads which ran explained that lucky win coupons had been inserted in the loaves of Vaughn's and that up to twenty-five dollars could be won in one loaf. The announcements concluded with a veiled reference to the free coupons in the stores with the phrase ''(n)o purchase necessary.''

The FCC decided that Vaughn's sales campaign was a lottery and that WBRE-TV had violated the federal law prohibiting the broadcast of information promoting lotteries.

It was clear that the first two lottery elements were satisfied by this promotion. Prizes were available (cash coupons up to $25 in value) and they were awarded on the basis of chance (the fortuity of choosing one loaf off the shelf rather than another). The third element, consideration, was more difficult and the Commission's reasoning in finding it here is one of the significant aspects of this case.

The phrase in the ads ''[n]o purchase necessary'' was not considered determinative on the issue of consideration.

Had the evidence shown that, in operation, those contestants not wishing to purchase the product were given the same chances to enter and win as those who bought the bread, there would have been no consideration. The FCC calls that its ''reasonably equal availability test,'' which requires that ''nonpurchasing contestants must be able to obtain chances in the same places, at the same times, and in the same number as purchasing contestants, in a setting which does not otherwise encourage a purchase.''[8]

However, it was discovered that those who did not buy Vaughn's bread were allowed only one free coupon by the grocers, whereas those who bought the bread could obtain an unlimited number of coupons by simply buying more than one loaf. On that basis, the FCC concluded that the element of consideration was shown and the sale campaign was a lottery.

Despite the violation of Section 1304, the station was not fined because of what the Commission admitted was this rather confusing twist to the often complex law of lotteries. As no prior FCC decision had explained the "reasonably equal availability test" and its relationship to consideration, and government felt it would be unfair to punish WBRE-TV for this violation.

Colorado Springs, Colorado

KEDI was fined $500.00 in 1973 for airing a Pizza Hut commercial which encouraged listeners to chew their way to a new wardrobe. The way the giveaway worked was that anyone who purchased a pizza would receive a pizza platter, many of which were stamped with the letters K, E, D or I. If any customer eventually collected all four platters, he or she would win a thirty dollar gift certificate at a clothing store.

The FCC categorized the pizza promotion as a lottery, finding all lottery elements present: prize (the gift certificate), chance (whether a customer received a K, E, D or I platter was obviously not dependent on skill, but rather luck) and consideration (only those buying pizzas could participate). And it fined the station for airing information about that illegal lottery in the form of ads for it.[9]

CHARITY PUBLIC SERVICE ANNOUNCEMENTS

Fort Worth, Texas

The local Holy Rosary Prayermen's Club raffled off a new Pontiac Firebird in 1968 to raise money for the Catholic schools in town. Tickets for the drawing were sold for a dollar each.

The prayer club approached radio station KOKA and requested its help in promoting the raffle. The station agreed to air a series of free public service announcments. Those PSA's alerted KOKA listeners that "(t)he Holy Rosary Prayermen Club is giving away a Pontiac Firebird on the 24th, and you can get your . . . dollar tickets, at Palais Royal and Bostian's Record Shop."[10]

The FCC classified the raffle as a lottery as its evidence showed all three definitional elements had been met. A prize was offered (the car); it was awarded on the basis of chance (the luck of the random drawing); and consideration was required to enter (the dollar raffle ticket).

In response to the station's defense that there could be nothing improper about encouraging a charitable donation to a needy parochial school, the Commission retorted that the PSA plainly and simply violated the lottery statute and that no distinction was made in the law for charitable lotteries. The government concluded the station must be punished even though it thought it was doing a good deed by donating air time to a worthy cause.

A short-term license renewal of one year was imposed due in part to other licensee misconduct, including logging violations and plugola conflicts of interest in addition to the lottery advertising.

Bakersfield, California

Each year, the Junior Baseball Association in this southern California town sponsored a barbeque at the local park to raise money. In 1972, the event featured music by the Kern River Blue Grass Boys and a drawing for a Motorola color television. Donations of two dollars were asked of all those who attended the barbeque.

The baseball parents asked radio station KWAC to help them advertise the annual fund-raiser. The station agreed to do so, free of charge; and it subsequently broadcast a series of fifty public service announcements over thirteen days promoting the barbeque.

The FCC decided that the picnic in the park with its door prize drawing was a lottery and slapped a $2,000 fine on KWAC. Stunned, the station protested that the annual barbeque was a charitable event which raised money for a worthwhile civic purpose—to give the children of Bakersfield a chance to play baseball during the summer. Beyond that, it explained that it didn't even charge a penny to the Baseball Association to air those spots—that it donated the time out of a sense of obligation to the community and the public interest. Too, KWAC denied that the picnic was a lottery because the voluntary donations asked for at the door did not constitute consideration.

The FCC was unpersuaded. Hard-nosed, it ruled that the barbeque and drawing were indeed a lottery. It concluded that the donation requested was in reality an admission fee which definitely satisfied the elements of consideration, that a prize was offered (the TV set) and that it was awarded on the basis or chance (a random drawing). A classic lottery, in the government's eyes.

As to the argument KWAC presented about the charitable nature of the baseball barbeque, the Commission refused to make any exceptions or bend the law, firmly stating that "(t)he lottery statute creates no exemption for sanctioned or worthy lotteries."[11]

STATIONS' OWN PROMOTIONS

Winston-Salem, North Carolina

Radio station WAAA had a booth at the 1969 Dixie Classic Fair held at Winston-Salem. To encourage listeners to visit the booth, the station developed a contest for the fair. Thousands of area basketball schedules were printed and numbered serially.

The local Coca-Cola bottler helped pay for the schedules, which featured a Coke logo, a listing of all basketball games to be broadcast on WAAA during the season, and a lucky number.

During frequent remote broadcasts from the fair, the station would randomly select winning numbers. The numbers were announced on the air and posted at the WAAY booth. And those fair-goers whose basketball schedule numbers matched the numbers drawn would receive prizes.

After a lengthy investigation, the FCC charged that WAAA had sponsored and advertised a lottery. The station retorted that its fair promotion was definitely not a lottery because the basketball schedules were distributed free of charge and that therefore the essential element of consideration was absent.

The Commission ruled that since only those people who paid the one dollar admission to the fair could visit the broadcaster's booth and participate in the contest, that they had in fact given valuable consideration in order to be eligible to win.

Finding the other elements of prize and chance obviously satisfied, the agency concluded WAAA had violated Section 1304 of Title 18 of the U.S. Code and fined the station $2,000.[12]

A further noteworthy aspect of this case is that here the lottery was not only advertised by the station . . . it was conducted by the station as well. Such a situation is rather unique, given the fact that most station lottery penalties are for broadcasting information about some business sponsor's lottery. The point is that station promotions can also constitute lotteries and, when they do, those stations will be held accountable.

PROGRAMS THAT AIRED

Los Angeles, California

On Saturday nights in 1955, KTLA-TV broadcast a TV Bingo show which it called "Play Marko." During the week, viewers would obtain Bingo cards from local businesses which sponsored the show.

During the telecast, the emcee would draw numbers from a cage and the players would mark the corresponding numbers on their cards at home. When anyone scored a Bingo, they would telephone the station. At that point, KTLA would verify the win by checking the serial number of the player's card against a master list of possible winning combinations. Prizes awarded included U.S. Savings Bonds, merchandise and a trip to Europe.

The program's producers sought a declaratory ruling from the FCC that the show was no lottery. The Commission decided just the opposite and found it in direct violation of Section 1304. Perplexed, the broadcaster argued that there was no charge for the Bingo cards and that viewers were not required to make purchases of any kind while in the stores to get their cards. The FCC responded that driving to and going into the stores to pick up Bingo cards was an expenditure of time and effort and therefore constituted the element of consideration. The other elements being obviously present (prize and chance), the FCC concluded "Play Marko" was a lottery.

The broadcaster simply couldn't accept the Commission's reasoning and appealed its decision to the U.S. Court of Appeals. That court reversed the FCC, holding that it would stretch the federal lottery statute to ridiculous lengths to characterize this TV show as a crime. The Judges refused to accept the premise that visiting a store to pick up a game card or an entry form constituted consideration. And "Play Marko" was allowed to continue on the air.[13]

Washington, D.C.

The lottery case involving radio station WOOK in the nation's capital is unique in many ways. In this case, the alleged broadcast lottery violation was not a station advertising some business sponsor's sales gimmick which turned out to be a lottery or a broadcaster plugging a charity's fund-raiser which even turned out to be a lottery. Here, regular programs on the licensee's schedule were found to have actually offered tips on the illegal numbers game operated by the underworld in the city. The kicker is that these were religious programs and sermons of area ministers.

The numbers game is a form of illegal gambling which involves people placing usually very meager bets (often a quarter and up to one dollar) on three-digit numbers. A winning number is chosen each day and it pays off.

WOOK's format was religious and it featured numerous programs consisting of sermons and services conducted by a variety of local ministers. An extensive FCC investigation and monitoring of tape recordings of those programs produced some shocking evidence that some ministers were offering tips to their listeners as to which three-digit number to choose each day in exchange for donations to their ministeries.

For a donation of $10.50, Queen Mother Ruby Etta Allen provided her followers with this tip on the air during a sermon: "God blessed the people three times from the blessing plan . . . [and] on Monday blessed on the 25th Psalm and on Psalm 71 and 9 on Wednesday."[14] The FCC noted that the winning number on Monday was 250 and on Wednesday was 719.

In one 1969 sermon, The Rev. James Belk spoke on the topic "a seed of prosperity." He intoned: "I told you how we would read our Psalm 60–62; Praise God, 62 and 6. I wanted you to read it, I wanted you to read it."[15] The winning number that day was 626.

A Bishop Bonner empathized with those in the audience who had been playing the numbers game for so long without any success. During a broadcast, he lamented: "(E)very day you try to win and you don't win. You put a little money here and you put a little money there and you don't win."[16] Then, he explained that the answer was to seek his help and in that way "be the most successful person in the game."[17]

The Rev. Dowell read this testimonial from one of his listeners on the air: "(t)he first time I came to see you, I was blessed for $135 for a quarter, and the second time I came I received $540 for a one dollar investment."[18]

The station tried to deflect responsibility by claiming that it had been itself victimized by the clever subterfuges of the broadcast ministers and that it was innocently unaware that any wrongdoing was afoot. The FCC growled back that only an incompetent and careless broadcaster would not have been alerted by the obviously suspicious remarks of the preachers on the air. It emphasized it was the broadcaster's duty to supervise its programs to eliminate any lottery information or references.

The government wasted little time in classifying the numbers game as a lottery as it easily satisfied the elements of prize (the money paid off each day), chance (the winning three-digit number was randomly selected) and consideration (those wishing to play placed bets of at least a quarter).

For violating Section 1304 by airing several different programs which contained lottery information, WOOK's license was flat out revoked by the FCC.

As this case represents the most severe sanction ever meted out by the Commission for a lottery violation, it merits further analysis. To be sure, broadcasters should be on notice that breaches of the lottery laws during commercials and PSA's will be treated more gently than those during actual programs. Management must indeed closely supervise especially all local programming to insure that no lottery information is aired. Producers, directors and even those on the cameras should be trained to spot lotteries and perhaps given a cash reward for every lottery they catch during taping.

The severity of the penalty in this particular WOOK case was probably dictated by the unusual fact that rather than a grocer's or hardware retailer's innocent sales promotion, the lottery at bottom here was in fact a big-time illegal gambling operation—the ultimate lottery. Broadcasters, while certainly maintaining lottery vigilance, can take some comfort in the knowledge that the FCC has made a determined and conscious effort to redress lottery violations with fines only. It was only in this rarest and most outrageous of cases that the Commission resorted to its harshest sanction.

1. 18 U.S.C. § 1304 (1982).

2. 47 C.F.R. § 73.1211 (1983).

3. *WFMY Television Corporation,* 50 FCC 2d 1168 (1975).

4. *Thomasville Broadcasting Company,* 50 FCC 2d 949 (1975); *WMFR, Incorporated,* 50 FCC 2d 963 (1975).

5. *Metromedia, Inc.,* et al., 60 FCC 2d 1075 (1976).

6. *V.I. Industries, Inc.,* 47 FCC 2d 271 (1974); *V.I. Industries, Inc.,* 49 FCC 2d 1031 (1974).

7. *DAE Broadcasting Company,* 40 FCC 2d 107 (1973); *DAE Broadcasting Company,* 42 FCC 2d 872 (1973).

8. *WBRE-TV Inc.,* 18 FCC 2d 96, 99 (1969).

9. *Garden of the Gods Broadcasting Company,* 43 FCC 2d 554 (1973).

10. *KOKA Broadcasting Co., Inc.,* 28 FCC 2d 41, 43 (1971).

11. *KMAP, Inc.,* 44 FCC 2d 971, 972 (1974).

12. *Laury Associates, Inc.,* 27 FCC 2d 870 (1971).

13. *Caples Company v. United States,* 243 F.2d 232 (D.C. Cir. 1957).

14. *United Television Co., Inc.,* et al., 55 FCC 2d 431, 441 (1973). [Initial Decision of Administrative Law Judge Forest L. McClenning].

15. *Ibid.,* 442.

16. *United Television Co., Inc.,* et al., 55 FCC 2d 416, 420 (1975).

17. *Ibid.*

18. *Ibid.,* 421.

CHAPTER 17

The Lottery Laws: What Broadcasters Must Do

To gain a working understanding of their lottery obligations, broadcasters must wade through a swamp of legal technicalities.

The Fine Print

Two of the three definitional lottery elements—prize and chance—have always been easy for broadcasters to spot. When anything of value is offered in a promotion to a customer or contestant—be it a free bag of Doritos or a Buick—that's a prize. And when the winner of the game is selected by luck rather than skill or knowledge, chance is involved. Contests where skill determines the winners would include writing competitions such as those requiring contestants to describe something in twenty-five words or less, or to name a new product or develop a slogan for a city's centennial. Blind luck, however, is all that a contestant would need to win a card drawing or promotion where the 1,000th customer to walk through the supermarket's cash register lane won a turkey.

The third lottery element—that of consideration—has, on the other hand, remained much more illusive. For sure, if a contestant must furnish anything of value in order to participate in the game or promotion, consideration has been met. But the problem has always been deciding what constitutes "something of value."

Contests requiring things of value which have been found to constitute consideration include:

- if the contestant must purchase a product and have it in his/her possession;

- if a boxtop from that product is submitted as the contest entry blank;

- if entry forms are available only to those customers purchasing a product;

- if the contestant must expend substantial time and energy to compete.

Contests where no consideration has been found:

- if the contestant can submit a facsimile boxtop or other product identification (e.g. an index card with the name of the product written on it) in lieu of purchasing the product and sending in an entry form off its box;

- if entry forms are available to all who enter the store whether or not they purchase a product;

- if the contestant need expend only minimal time and energy to compete (for instance, drive to a store to register for a contest or watch a television program at home in order to be able to answer questions when called on the telephone).

- if all the contestant need buy is a stamp or postcard to send in an entry.

- if the money required to be furnished by a contestant to enter is paid to someone other than the business which is promoting and sponsoring the contest. (For instance, if a radio station sponsors a golf giveaway and contestants are required only to pay green fees to local courses and then mail their scorecards into the station for selection on the basis of random drawing. In this situation, the consideration (green fees) were not paid to the contest's sponsor (the station), nor did golfing skill determine the winner. The luck of the random draw did.

Defenses Rejected by the FCC

The following is a list of defenses or excuses raised in a series of cases by broadcast stations charged with violating the federal lottery laws. Each was flatly rejected by the FCC.

1. The station did not intend to violate the lottery laws.[1]

2. The station had been assured by the ad agency which placed the lottery spot that "the copy was cleared by an attorney."[2] In another case, the attorney for the business which ran the lottery ad advised that the copy was satisfactory.[3]

3. Ineffective management, inattention of management, personnel problems and the inability of the owner to employ replacement management quickly enough

made it impossible for the station to follow its customary screening procedures for advertising and the lottery slipped through. Specifically here, "(t)he former manager . . . was . . . campaigning for the Virgin Islands' Senate at the time these announcements had been run."[4] And, the next manager hired died ten days later.

4. The licensee did not know that a purchase of a bottle of Scotch was necessary to participate in the drawing (thus satisfying the lottery element of consideration) because the ad agency handling the matter did not so inform the broadcaster.[5]

5. The sales campaign was produced and approved by a well-known Fortune 500 national corporation (the Pepsi Cola Company) and broadcast across the country on numerous local stations. Therefore, the station assumed it was lawful.[6]

6. The station employee who accepted what turned out to be a lottery ad was inexperienced, did not normally make such decisions regarding sponsors and ad copy, and simply made an honest mistake.[7]

7. Key management personnel were absent from the station the day the lottery ads were aired.[8]

8. The lottery ad was run for only a short period of time and the prize offered was a nominal fifty dollars.[9]

9. The lottery advertising which subjected the station to a $500 forfeiture grossed the station only twelve dollars when it was aired.[10]

10. The station's general manager was severely paralyzed as a result of polio and that job was one of the few he could perform. For those reasons, he wouldn't inten-

tionally violate any FCC rule which "might jeopardize"[11] his career.

11. The lottery laws are a "cloudy and uncertain segment of the law"[12] and the station took every conceivable step to comply with what it understood to be its obligations.

12. The continuity director responsible for reviewing the ad copy did not even know what a lottery was.[13]

13. The station, located in the state of North Carolina, reported that the "best legal minds in North Carolina"[14] can't figure out the broadcast lottery laws.

Penalties for Broadcasting Lotteries

The strict letter of the law makes broadcasters vulnerable to criminal prosecution and imprisonment for violating the federal lottery statute. However, that has never occured; and the government has contented itself with the FCC adjudicating such cases and imposing the lesser civil penalties at its disposal.

Any of the Commission's sanctions are available to it in redressing lottery violations—revocation of license, short-term renewal of license, forfeiture, censure or admonition. FCC penalties in these cases could be severe because lottery broadcasts violate the U.S. Code, FCC Rules and the public interest obligation which every station owes.

As the first and foremost duty imposed on all licensees and as the very core of the Communications Act of 1934,[15] the obligation to operate in the public interest is the one which all broadcasters know the FCC is consumed with. Its premise is that the airwaves should be used to benefit the public and meet the public's interests, and never be used to threaten the public health, morality or well-being. When a broadcaster airs a lottery announcement, in the FCC's book it encourages illegality and gambling—which is indeed adverse to the well-being and morality of the public. And when that agency concludes one of its licensees has breached the public interest obligation, fire blazes from its nostrils. Licenses are taken back, stations are hit, fines are slapped on and careers in broadcasting are shattered. It is a cardinal rule of broadcasting that the last thing a station can chance is to violate that public interest standard.

Relevant to this chapter is the cold fact that the FCC has ruled that lottery broadcasts violate the public interest obligation in all of five different ways. Specifically, the government has determined such broadcasts violate the United States Criminal Code [18 U.S.C. § 1304] and specific FCC Rules [47 C.F.R. § 73.1211]; that they contravene the FCC's long-established policy that its licensees not aid illegal gambling; that those programs encourage poor ghetto listeners and viewers to spend their money on bets and tips, thus aggravating their plight; that the coffers of organized crime are filled; and that the broadcasts constitute false, misleading and deceptive advertising.[16] Quintuplets. Not good news for stations which know that violating the public interest in even one way—let alone five—can result in the loss of a license.

So, the potential for real damage is there; and a station's window of vulnerability is indeed wide. Yet, the FCC has displayed moderation and restraint in meting out lottery penalties. Virtually all violators have been merely fined.

The forfeiture procedure a licensee would face in this situation is as follows. First, the FCC staff would investigate the allegations that a station carried a lottery announcement. All available evidence would be sought and studied. If the facts warranted, the Commission would then issue a Notice of Apparent Liability noting the results of the investigation and setting a fine in a specific dollar amount. Such a Notice would be sent to the station by certified mail.

Upon receipt of the Notice, several options would be available to the licensee. It could, within thirty days, file a statement with the FCC denying that it broadcast a lottery and providing the agency with all corroborating evidence. The FCC would then review the station's arguments and either relieve it of liability or issue an order of forfeiture requiring it to pay the fine. Or, the station could admit that it broadcast a lottery but present reasons to the Commission within thirty days why the fine imposed in the Notice should be reduced. The FCC would in that event reconsider the facts and decide whether to lessen the fine. Or, the station could do nothing in response to the Notice. In that case, after thirty days, the FCC would issue an order for forfeiture for the amount listed in the Notice payable to the Treasurer of the United States.[17]

News of Lotteries

The federal lottery statute, it will be recalled, prohibits "the broadcasting of, any advertisement of *or information concerning any lottery.*"[18] (emphasis supplied) To what extent news stories relating to lotteries constitute untouchable "information concerning" them is a question the FCC and the courts have addressed. Typically, the only aspects of any lottery most broadcasters consider newsworthy are those involving the results and operations of state-operated lotteries within their own states. Who won a two dollar discount on a pair of designer jeans at the Pants Corral in that business's sales promotion lottery is simply never news. So, the focus has been on state lotteries; and several clear guidelines have been issued detailing what stations can and cannot broadcast.

State Lottery News Which Can Be Broadcast

1.   Legitimate news stories involving newsworthy events of current interest in the lottery's operation (for exam-

ple, a report of a state legislator's proposal to exempt lottery winnings from state taxes or a story describing how lottery proceeds are distributed or a human interest story on lottery winners);

2. Live broadcasts or later reports of speeches or statements made by public officials which comment on and even praise lotteries;

3. Interviews with lottery winners (including such questions as what do you plan to do with the money, how many tickets did you purchase and what was your immediate reaction upon being told you had won?);

4. Documentary programs which explain how the lotteries operate and present the views of both those who favor lotteries and those who oppose them;

5. Station editorial on lotteries;

6. Panel discussions of lotteries;

7. Reports or documentaries on illegal lotteries and illegal gambling in the area.[19]

State Lottery News Which Cannot Be Broadcast

1. Long lists of winners;

2. Reports containing information on where, how and when lottery tickets may be purchased;

3. Reports noting where the winning tickets will be drawn;

4. Live broadcasts of the drawing of winning lottery tickets.[20]

The distinction between the two categories above is that the news stories in the second, prohibited group directly promote existing state lotteries and are therefore made unlawful by the court's interpretation of the lottery statute. Those news reports in the first group are considered to only incidentally and indirectly promote lotteries and are tolerated on that basis.

The Exception for State-conducted Lotteries

On January 2, 1975, the Congress amended the federal lottery statute to permit some broadcast stations to advertise or carry information concerning some official state lotteries.[21] The lawmakers were responding to the pleas of broadcasters in the states which operated legal, revenue generating, ticket selling lotteries such as the Illinois State Lottery and New York State Lottery.

Under the terms of this exception, two types of broadcast stations can advertise or carry information concerning an official state lottery. First, those stations licensed to communities inside any state which operates an official lottery. Second, if a licensee operates in a state with an official lottery, it can also run ads and carry information concerning the state lotteries of any adjacent state.

The FCC Rules and Regulations have also been revised to reflect this Congressional amendment.[22]

Just When You Thought it Was Safe Enough to Come Out of the Control Booth . . . More Lottery Laws to Follow

For starters, it is clear by now that all broadcast stations must comply with the federal anti-lottery laws or face a wide range of penalties. Since radio and television stations are licensed by the federal government, most grudgingly accept regulation of their operations by the bureaucrats in Washington. And everything that has been written so far about what types of business sales promotions and charitable events constitute lotteries stands as the front line of battle as the licensee attempts to meet its lottery obligations.

A second front has developed, however, in the lottery war: several state governments have enacted anti-lottery broadcasting statutes. And the absolutely exasperating part of it is that the states can't agree with each other on what constitutes a lottery and some states even disagree with the FCC's definition of what conduct meets the lottery elements. In some states, a certain business sales promotion is an illegal lottery while in other states it is not. In some states, a particular charitable fund-raising scheme is by law not a lottery while at the federal level it is.

Most of the disagreement involves the element of consideration. While virtually all state governments accept the three element definition of a lottery, there appears to be no agreement as to what constitutes consideration. In some states, only the expenditure of money by the contestant to participate in the game satisfies consideration. In others, the expenditure of effort alone constitutes consideration. Thus, in the latter group of states, even though a business promotion required no purchase of those who wished to participate and only asked that interested parties visit the store to pick up the free entry blank or bingo card, consideration would be met and the promotion would be considered an illegal lottery. Just the opposite result, of course, would attach in those states that required monetary consideration, such as the purchase of a certain brand of cereal in order to fill out a box top entry card.

Particularly vexing to many broadcasters is the harsh reality that some contests, games and giveaways easily pass FCC muster but not that of certain states. Since the FCC is the ultimate expert and official communications agency of the United States of America, with experience and knowledge which are unmatched and incomparable, just why isn't their definition of what constitutes consideration good enough for some distant state legislature that knows no more about broadcast station regulation than how to change channels on their TV sets at home?

A legal battle is now being waged over whether, in fact, the federal government and FCC have preempted the whole area of broadcast lottery law and are the only ones who can impose lottery obligations on radio and TV stations. It could be years before that question is resolved. In the meantime, broadcasters must resign themselves to doing lottery battle on two fronts against two different armies. When fighting on the federal front, broadcasters must use the FCC's lottery definition. When fighting on the state front, that state's interpretation is controlling.

To even understand why the state governments worry about lotteries and go out of their way to do lottery battle with broadcasters, history must be consulted. The fact is that most state lottery laws were originally enacted to prohibit the types of illegal gambling often associated with organized crime—specifically, the numbers game and the running of policy slips. The states, responsible for the welfare of their citizens, acted to protect the people from squandering their money in schemes that were nearly impossible to win. It was, then, a wave of anti-gambling spirit which moved state legislatures to enact broadcast lottery laws prohibiting the advertising of lotteries or the airing of any lottery information in their states.

A few states have recently liberalized their lottery statutes to allow legitimate business sales promotions and charitable raffles. But, of course, such a breakthrough on the state front is not applicable on the federal front where such activities clearly remain illegal to broadcast.

To effectively do battle on the state front, each broadcaster must know the enemy. The only way to do that is to locate and read the lottery statute of the state in which the station is licensed. A list of all those state laws is included as a footnote to this chapter.[23]

On the federal front, the army of regulators at the FCC is primarily responsible for the lottery war. There are other federal combatants, too, which should be identified as we overview the battle zone. Note, however, that their threat is essentially directed at those businesses and charities which sponsor illegal lotteries. The U.S. Postal Service enforces various laws which makes it a crime to mail lottery materials. The Federal Trade Commission's (FTC) Rules prohibit lotteries by grocers or gas stations unless certain contest information is disclosed, including the odds of winning and the number of prizes. In the FTC's view, these lotteries are unfair methods of competition and the agency can impose cease and desist orders against their sponsors. While a broadcast station could be subject to such FTC penalties if it sponsored or co-sponsored such a lottery, it is primarily the business sponsors who incur the FTC's wrath.[24]

What Broadcasters Must Do

Generally, the obligation the FCC imposes is that all licensees must exercise reasonable diligence, control and supervision of their employees and of their programming to ensure that no lottery announcements are broadcast.[25]

In meeting that obligation, broadcasters are expected to scrutinize every commercial and public service announcement the station plans to air. This is true even if the ad is placed through a heavy volume agency or big name advertiser which assures the station that the ad copy is free from lottery taint. Trained and careful station personnel must sniff, poke at and test every commercial for lottery traces. The station should be suspicious of all announcements and be hard-nosed in its approach.

To get the job done at the station and to sound lottery battle stations for the employees, an active lottery campaign is advisable. The licensee should adopt a clearly worded station policy against lotteries and vigorously enforce it. Management and staff should be sensitized to the importance of keeping lotteries off the licensee's air. And a continuing training program should be developed to educate all station employees about lotteries and how to spot them.

Beyond those several responsibilities at the station, a licensee's lottery duties extend to the shopping malls and downtown business districts. For the FCC has made it plain that stations must also satisfy themselves that, in actual day-to-day operation, the business sales promotion or seemingly innocent charity event being advertised is not being conducted as an illegal lottery.[26]

Stations must verify that the promotions, give-aways or contests they are asked to advertise are not lotteries. An acceptable investigation would involve the ad salesman visiting the sponsor's place of business to make such a determination or a continuity director telephoning the sponsor to ask if the scheme included the elements of prize, chance and consideration. It would be insufficient for the station merely to ask the ad agency which placed the spot whether a lottery lurked behind the copy.

Why Is This Illegal, Anyway?

All right, so we understand it now. It's a crime for a local TV or radio station to carry an ad for a supermarket or gas station if the give-away or register-to-win game it promotes involves prize, chance and consideration. And it's a crime for a station to air a public service announcement for a church or civic group if their raffle or fund-raiser being promoted is in operation a lottery. But, why?

Explaining how all of this makes sense is probably impossible because such an undertaking assumes that it does make sense. But the justification is historical; and today's FCC prosecutions and fines are the result of deeply engrained public policies and the will of Congress that span literally two centuries.

First, understand what is being done here. The federal lottery laws do not prohibit lotteries as such. However, the Congress has taken strong action to inhibit lotteries by denying their promoters access to those instrumentalities which the federal government controls. In fact, the federal lottery laws prohibit the mailing of lottery advertising, materials or information,[27] the importation or interstate shipment of lottery materials,[28] the sale of lotteries by or other participation by federally-insured banks and savings and loan associations,[29] and the broadcast of lottery advertising or information on any federally-licensed radio or television station.[30]

These are anti-gambling laws which deny gamblers the modes of interstate commerce to ply their trade. Some were enacted as long ago as 1827[31] and were designed, in the opinion of one early federal judge, "to protect the [private] citizen from the demoralizing or corrupting influence"[32] of solicitations to gamble.

In an 1830 speech, a member of the Pennsylvania legislature intoned that "the lottery destroys the happiness of the poor by its false hopes, draws them away from labor and industry and leads to pauperism, misery and crime."[33] An 1850 United States Supreme Court decision railed against the "pestilence of lotteries . . . [which] infests the whole community. It . . . preys upon the hard earnings of the poor; it plunders the ignorant and the simple."[34]

Lotteries have been branded by history as immoral, contrary to public policy and threats to the public welfare. As the Washington Supreme Court observed in 1969, laws prohibiting lotteries "are designed to prevent the public from wagering their substance upon chance and fortuitous events so that one cannot be enticed to hazard his earnings on a chance to win a prize."[35] Throughout history, lottery laws have been enacted to prohibit the numbers games and policy slips gambling often associated with organized crime. The rationale was to protect the public from squandering its money.

When the Congress brought all radio stations under federal licensing control and established the FCC by approving the Communications Act of 1934, it included an anti-lottery provision banning their broadcast. That was known in 1934 as Section 316 of the Act and it became Section 1304 of the U.S. Criminal Code in 1948 when Title 18 of the Code was revised.[36] The point is that since the earliest days of broadcast regulation, lottery programs and announcements have been prohibited.

The FCC took the baton and in 1952 launched a campaign to revoke the licenses of stations which aired then-popular give-away programs like ABC's ''Stop The Music'' and NBC's ''What's My Name.'' Those shows gave listeners and viewers the chance to win merchandise by correctly answering game questions when telephoned at home during the show. But they were lotteries, by God, stormed the FCC—''the old lottery evil under a new guise, and . . . they should be struck down as illegal devices appealing to cupidity and the gambling spirit.''[37]

Characterizing such give-aways as ''illicit appendages to legitimate advertising,''[38] the Commission faulted them for appealing to ''the gambling spirit—the lure of obtaining something for nothing or almost nothing.''[39] In this case, the FCC was overruled and restrained by the Supreme Court which decided those programs were definitionally not lotteries because they did not require consideration to participate or compete.

But, is the manager of the Western Auto store who gives away a flashlight to the 600th customer really running a gambling establishment? Is the housewife who registers at the A & P for a free Thanksgiving turkey actually gambling illegally? Or, instead, are most of these so called lotteries really innocent, good faith forms of advertising and customer solicitation? And what shopper puts his or her paycheck on the line at the Dairy Queen to submit an entry in a free banana split drawing? Is this, in truth, gambling? I say it isn't and that the historical justifications for prohibiting these broadcasts have rusted through time. Today, innocent business advertisers and charities are being snared in a legal minefield set for gangsters and racketeers. This isn't right and it makes no sense.

Recognizing the inappropriateness of subjecting at least charitable lotteries to the broadcast ban, the U.S. Senate in 1978 voted to carve out an exception for them and allow their promotion on radio and TV stations. The House did not act on the bill, however, and the measure died in the 95th Congress.[40] And while several states have moved to allow innocent business sales promotions and charitable fundraising lotteries within their borders, federally-licensed broadcast stations in those states are still obligated to adhere to the stricter federal prohibition. But, somehow, it just doesn't seem right.

NOTES/17

1. *DAE Broadcasting Company,* 40 FCC 2d 107 (1973).

2. *University of Florida,* 40 FCC 2d 188 (1973).

3. *Taft Broadcasting Company,* 18 FCC 2d 186 (1969).

4. *V.I. Industries, Inc.,* 47 FCC 2d 271, 272 (1974).

5. *Ibid.*

6. *Lawrence Broadcasters, Inc.,* 14 FCC 2d 384 (1968).

7. *Gaffney Broadcasting, Inc.,* 23 FCC 2d 912 (1970).

8. *WFMY Television Corp.,* 50 FCC 2d 1168 (1975).

9. *Call of Houston, Inc.,* 12 FCC 2d 733 (1968).

10. *Ohio Quests, Inc.,* 8 FCC 2d 859 (1967).

11. *Williamsburg County Broadcasting, Inc.,* 30 FCC 2d 173, 174 (1971).

12. *Taft Broadcasting Company,* 18 FCC 2d 186 (1969).

13. *Hertz Broadcasting of Birmingham, Inc.,* et al., 54 FCC 2d 74 (1975). [Initial Decision of Administrative Law Judge James F. Tierney]

14. *Thomasville Broadcasting Company,* 50 FCC 2d 919 (1975).

15. 47 U.S.C. §§ 301, 307, 308, 309 (1982).

16. *United Television Company, Inc.,* et al., 20 FCC 2d 278, 279 at note 2 (1969).

17. 47 C.F.R. § 1.80 (1983); 47 U.S.C. §§ 503(b) (1)(B) and (C) (1982); 47 U.S.C. § 503(b)(2) (1982); 47 U.S.C. § 509 (1982).

   See Chapter 8 for a further analysis and discussion of the forfeiture penalty.

18. 18 U.S.C. § 1304 (1982).

19. *Lotteries,* 21 FCC 2d 846 (1970); *New York State Broadcasters Ass'n v. United States,* 414 F.2d 990 (2nd Cir. 1969).

20. *Ibid.*

21. 18 U.S.C. § 1307 (1982).

22. *State Conducted Lotteries,* 51 FCC 2d 173 (1975).

23. ALABAMA: ALA. CONST., art. IV, § 65; ALA. CODE § 13A-12-20 (1982).

   ALASKA: ALASKA STAT. §§ 11.66.200, .210, .220, .230, .240, .250, .260, .270, .280 (1983); ALASKA STAT. §§ 05.15.200, .210 (1981).

   ARIZONA: ARIZ. REV. STAT. ANN. § 13-3304 (1983).

   ARKANSAS: ARK. CONST., art. 19, § 14; ARK. STAT. ANN. §§ 41-3272, -3273, -3274, -3275, -3276, -3277 (1947).

   CALIFORNIA: CAL. CONST., art. 4, § 26; CAL. PENAL CODE §§ 319, 320, 321, 322, 323, 324 (West 1970); CAL. PENAL CODE §§ 326.5, 328 (West 1984).

   COLORADO: COLO. CONST., art. XVIII, § 2; COLO. REV. STAT. §§ 18-10-101, -102 (1973); COLO. REV. STAT. §§ 12-9-101, -102 (1978)

   CONNECTICUT: CONN. GEN. STAT. ANN. §§ 7-169, -179 (West 1972); CONN. GEN. STAT. ANN. §§ 53-290, -293 (West 1960).

   DELAWARE: DEL. CONST., art. 2, § 17; DEL. CODE ANN. tit. 29, §§ 4806, 4807, 4808, 4809, 4810 (1974)

   DISTRICT OF COLUMBIA: D.C. CODE §§ 22-1501, -1516, -1517, -1518 (1981).

   FLORIDA: FLA. CONST., art. 10, § 7; FLA. STAT. ANN. §§ 849.09, 849.092, 849.093, 849.094 (West 1976).

   GEORGIA: GA. CONST., art. I, § II; GA. CODE ANN. §§ 26-2701, 26-2702, 26-2705, 26-2714 (1983).

HAWAII: HAWAII REV. STAT. §§ 712-1220, 712-1221 (1976).

IDAHO: IDAHO CONST., art. 3, § 20; IDAHO CODE §§ 18-4901, 18-4902, 18-4904 (1979).

ILLINOIS: ILL. CONST., art. IV, § 27; ILL. ANN. STAT. ch. 38, § 28-1 (Smith-Hurd 1983); ILL. ANN. STAT. ch. 38, § 28-2 (Smith-Hurd 1977).

INDIANA: IND. CONST., art. 15, § 8; IND. CODE ANN. § 35-45-5-1 (Burns 1979).

IOWA: IOWA CONST., art. 3, § 29; IOWA CODE §§ 99B.1, 99B.7, 99B.8, 99B.11, 725.7, 725.12, 725.15, 725.16 (1983).

KANSAS: KANSAS CONST., art. 15, § 3; KANSAS STAT. ANN. §§ 21-4302, 21-4303, 21-4304, 21-4305 (1981).

KENTUCKY: KY. CONST., § 226: KY. REV. STAT. ANN. §§ 436.420, 528.010, 528.020, 528.030 (Bobbs-Merrill 1975).

LOUISIANA: LA. CONST., art. 19, § 8; LA. REV. STAT. ANN. §§ 4861.1, 4861.3, 4861.4 (1983).

MAINE: ME. REV. STAT. ANN. tit. 17, §§ 324, 330 (1983).

MARYLAND: MD. CONST., art. III, § 36; MD. ANN. CODE art. 27, §§ 356, 369, 369A (1982).

MASSACHUSETTS: MASS. GEN. LAWS ANN. ch. 271, §§ 6c, 7A, 8 (West 1983).

MICHIGAN: MICH. STAT. ANN. §§ 28.604, 28.605, 28.607 (Callaghan 1982).

MINNESOTA: MINN. CONST., art. 13 § 5; MINN. STAT. ANN. § 609.75 (West 1983).

MISSISSIPPI: MISS. CONST., art. 4, § 98; MISS. CODE ANN. §§ 97-33-33, 97-33-35, 97-33-37, 97-33-49 (1973); MISS.CODE ANN. § 97-33-51 (1983).

MISSOURI: MO. CONST., art. 3, § 39; MO. ANN. STAT. § 572.030 (Vernon 1979).

MONTANA: MONT. CONST., art. XIX, § 2; MONT. CODE ANN. §§ 23-5-201, 23-5-202, 23-5-205 (1983).

NEBRASKA: NEB. CONST., art. III, § 24; NEB. REV. STAT. §§ 28-1101, 28-1102, 28-1114, 28-1115 (1979).

NEVADA: NEV. CONST., art. 4, § 24; NEV. REV. STAT. §§ 462.010, 462.020 (1980).

NEW HAMPSHIRE: N.H. REV. STAT. ANN. §§ 287-A, 287-B (1966); N.H. REV. STAT. ANN. §§ 287-D:1, 287-D:2 (1981).

NEW JERSEY: N.J. CONST., art. 4, § 7; N.J. STAT. ANN. §§ 2c:37-1, 2c:37-2 (West 1982).

NEW MEXICO: N.M. STAT. ANN. §§ 30-19-1, 30-19-2 (1978); N.M. STAT. ANN. § 30-19-6 (1983).

NEW YORK: N.Y. CONST., art. 1, § 9; N.Y. PENAL LAW § 225.00 (McKinney 1980).

NORTH CAROLINA: N.C. GEN. STAT. §§ 14-289, 14-290, 14-292 (1981).

NORTH DAKOTA: N.D. CONST., art. XI, § 25; N.D. CENT. CODE §§ 12.1-28.01, 12.1-28.02 (1983).

OHIO: OHIO CONST., art. XV, § 6; OHIO REV. CODE ANN. §§ 2915.01, 2915.02, 2915.07 (Page 1982).

OKLAHOMA: OKLA. STAT. ANN. tit. 21, §§ 1051, 1052, 1053, 1056 (West 1983).

OREGON: OR. CONST., art. XV, § 4; OR. REV. STAT. §§ 167.117, 167.127 (1981).

PENNSYLVANIA: PA. STAT. ANN. tit. 18, §§ 5512, 5513 (Purdon 1983).

RHODE ISLAND: R.I. CONST., art. XLI, § 1; R.I. GEN. LAWS §§ 11-19-1, 11-19-30.1 (1981).

SOUTH CAROLINA: S.C. CONST., art. 17, § 7; S.C. CODE ANN. §§ 16-19-10, 16-19-20 (Law. Co-op. 1977).

SOUTH DAKOTA: S.D. CONST., art. III, § 25; S.D. CODI-FIED LAWS ANN. §§ 22-25-24, 22-25-25, 22-25-26 (1979).

TENNESSEE: TENN. CONST., art. 11, § 5; TENN. CODE ANN. §§ 39-6-601, 39-6-607, 39-6-609, 39-6-624 (1982).

TEXAS: TEX. CONST., art. 3, § 47; TEX. PENAL CODE ANN. §§ 47.01, 47.02 (Vernon 1982).

UTAH: UTAH CONST., art. VI, § 27; UTAH CODE ANN. §§ 76-10-1101, 76-10-1102, 76-10-1104 (1978).

VERMONT: VT. STAT. ANN. tit. 13, §§ 2101, 2102, 2103 (1974).

VIRGINIA: VA. CONST., art. IV, § 60; VA. CODE § 18.2-242 (1982).

WASHINGTON: WASH. CONST., art. 2, § 24; WASH. REV. CODE ANN. § 9.46.020 (1977).

WEST VIRGINIA: W. VA. CONST., art. 6, § 36; W. VA. CODE §§ 61-10-11, 61-10-11a (1977).

WISCONSIN: WIS. CONST., art. 4, § 24; WIS. STAT. ANN. §§ 945.01, 945.02, 945.03 (1982)

WYOMING: WYO. STAT. ANN. §§ 6-7-101, 6-7-102 (1983).

24. Trade Regulation Rule, Part 419—*Games of Chance in the Food Retailing and Gasoline Industries. Statement of Basis and Purpose of Trade Regulation Rule,* 34 Fed. Reg. 13302 (1969); 2 Trade Reg. Rep. 7975 (1969).

25. *Folkways Broadcasting Co., Inc.,* et al., 48 FCC 2d 739 (1972).

26. *Metromedia, Inc.*, et al., 60 FCC 2d 1075, 1982–83 (1976); *Meredith Colon Johnston*, et al., 1 FCC 2d 720 (1965).

27. 18 U.S.C. § 1302 (1982).

28. 18 U.S.C. § 1301 (1982).

29. 18 U.S.C. § 1306 (1982).

30. 18 U.S.C. § 1304 (1982).

31. 4 Stat. 238, 239 (1827). (A prohibition on using the U.S. mails to conduct lotteries.)

32. *United States v. Horner*, 44 F. 677, 679 (S.D.N.Y. 1891); *aff'd* 143 U.S. 207 (1892).

33. F. Williams, *Flexible Participation Lotteries* 6, note 6 (1938). [Quoting McMaster, *History Of The People Of The U.S.*, Vol. 7, p 154 (1910)]

34. *Phalen v. Virginia*, 49 U.S. (8 How.) 163, 168 (1850).

35. *Schillberg v. Safeway Stores, Inc.*, 450 P.2d 949, 956 (Wash. 1969).

36. *F.C.C. v. American Broadcasting Co.*, 347 U.S. 284, 292 n.9 (1954).

37. *Ibid.*, 296.

38. *Ibid.*, 291.

39. *Ibid.*

40. 124 Cong. Rec. S.854 (daily ed. Jan. 30, 1978); S. 1437, 95th Cong., 2d Sess. (1978), 124 Cong. Rec. S. 860 (daily ed. Jan. 30, 1978). Congressional Quarterly, Dec. 8, 1979 at 2792.

CHAPTER 18

The Bottom Line: A Checklist to Avoid Problems

A. A Licensee Must:

For Contests

1. Adopt a detailed station contest integrity policy forbidding any false, misleading or deceptive contest activity [including advertising or promotion of the contest] or any contest dishonesty whatever.[1]

2. Insist that all station employees read and understand the contest policy.[2]

3. Closely supervise and control all employees to insure their full compliance with the contest policy, including monitoring the contest statements deejays make on the air.[3]

4. Fully disclose the material terms of the contest to the public, and explain all contest rules.[4]

5. Conduct the contest substantially as announced and advertised.[5]

6. Eliminate any false, misleading or deceptive contest advertising.[6]

7. Satisfy itself, after an active examination, that all advertising copy is accurate and honest; and carefully word all contest promos and clues so as not to mislead.[7]

8. Award all prizes within a reasonable time.[8]

9. Meet an exemplary standard of conduct in contest-type programs.[9]

10. Review the FCC's contest rules with new employees.[10]

11. Keep detailed records of each contest's ads, winners, prizes and rules.[11]

12. Maintain strict in-house contest security measures.[12]

13. Satisfy itself that even contests produced outside the station meet the station's contest integrity guidelines in every respect.[13]

14. File an I.R.S. Form 1099-MISC. for each contestant who wins a prize valued at $600 or more; and include as station income for tax purposes any money generated by a contest, including advertising revenue.[14]

15. Contact an attorney immediately upon receipt of any "Notice of Designation for Hearing" which contains a contest allegation. If the station does not file an answer within twenty days, it forfeits the right to be heard on the charges.[15]

For Lotteries

1. Scrutinize every commercial to ensure that the sponsor's game, giveaway or contest being advertised is not, in actual operation, an illegal lottery.[16]

2. Scrutinize every public service announcement to ensure that the charitable activity being promoted is not, in actual operation, an illegal lottery.[17]

3. Conduct in-store or telephone investigations of sponsor's or charities' games, giveaways, contests or raffles to verify that they are not being conducted as illegal lotteries.[18]

B. A Licensee Must Not:

For Contests

1. Prearrange or predetermine the outcome of a contest.[19]

2. Provide any special or secret assistance to particular contestants.[20]

3. Rig or fix a contest in order to predetermine the winners and losers.[21]

4. Describe any material contest term falsely, misleadingly or deceptively.[22]

5. Disseminate false or misleading prize information.[23]

6. Deny contestants a fair chance to win.[24]

7. Change the rules of a contest without notifying the public.[25]

8. Judge contest entries arbitrarily or capriciously.[26]

9. Employ hyperbole or exaggeration in advertising and promoting a contest.[27]

10. Improperly disqualify contestants even with the best of motives.[28]

11. Air any contest which creates an unreasonable risk of personal injury or property damage to the public.[29]

12. Broadcast either live or on a tape-delayed basis a telephone conversation with a contestant without informing that party and obtaining their consent.[30]

For Lotteries

1. Air a lottery, carry an advertisement for a lottery or broadcast any information about a lottery (except for official state lotteries in some states).[31]

C. A Licensee Should:

For Contests

1. Comply with any orders or requests of law enforcement officials regarding any contests.[32]

2. Conduct treasure hunts and other contests carefully so as not to violate others' property rights, threaten public safety, or divert police from other duties.[33]

3. Take all steps necessary to prevent contest improprieties.[34]

4. Ask all employees to attest that they have read and do understand the station's contest policy by signing their names to it.[35]

5. Quickly investigate any allegations of contest impropriety, insure the credibility and exhaustiveness of the investigation by selecting an attorney to conduct it, decisively punish any wrongdoing, act to eliminate its recurrence, and be the first to apprise the FCC of the problem.[36]

6. Upon being reliably informed of any contest misconduct, take responsibility and admit the error to the public in a special broadcast announcement or report.[37]

7. Be even more careful in its conduct of childrens' contests, as the FCC holds licensees to a higher childrens' standard of care.[38]

8. Instruct its bookkeeper or accountant to maintain a separate file or ledger page for each contest and take as tax deductions the costs of conducting any contest.

9. Require that prizewinners complete and sign a contest affidavit and contest prize receipt before receiving any prize.

For Lotteries

1. Adopt a clearly worded station policy against lotteries and vigorously enforce it.[39]

2. Develop a training program to educate all station employees about lotteries and how to spot them.[40]

Defenses Offered By Licensees and Rejected By the FCC:

In Contest Violation Cases

1. Lack of intent on the part of the licensee to mislead the public.[41]

2. Absence of owner or management knowledge of the employees' contest misconduct.[42]

3. The contest ads were technically not false, even though they were misleading.[43]

4. The improper contest was not produced or conducted by the licensee, but was purchased from a program syndicator or received from an independent source.[44]

5. The First Amendment protects station contests from FCC scrutiny.[45]

6. Absence of evidence of actual harm to the public.[46]

In Lottery Violation Cases

1. The station did not intend to violate the lottery laws.[47]

2. The station didn't know that the sponsor's giveaway was being conducted as an illegal lottery.[48]

3. The station made an honest mistake in accepting the lottery ad.[49]

4. The lottery laws are a "cloudy and uncertain segment of the law" and the station took every conceivable step to comply with what it understood to be its lottery obligations.[50]

5. A station located in North Carolina reported that it tried to obey the law but that even some of the ''best legal minds in North Carolina'' couldn't figure out the federal broadcast lottery obligations.[51]

1. *Bartell Broadcasting of Florida, Inc.*, 51 FCC 2d 2 (1974). *National Broadcasting Co., Inc.*, 25 FCC 2d 106 (1970).

2. *Walton Broadcasting, Inc.*, 78 FCC 2d 857 (1980).

3. *WMJX, Inc.*, 85 FCC 2d 251, 276 (1981). *KWK Radio, Inc.*, 34 FCC 1039, 1042 (1963). *WGOE, Inc.*, et al., 49 FCC 2d 327 (1974). *Centrum Corp.*, 36 Rad. Reg. 2d 201 (1976).

4. *United Broadcasting Company*, FCC 78-838, Mimeo decision 4530 (1978). *Notice of Proposed Rulemaking*, 40 Fed. Reg. 26692, June 25, 1975; and *Licensee-Conducted Contests*, 60 FCC 2d 1072 (1976). 47 C.F.R. § 73.1216 (1983).

5. *Oil Shale Broadcasting Company*, 68 FCC 2d 517 (1978). *Fox River Communications, Inc.*, 45 FCC 2d 1081 (1974). 47 C.F.R. § 73.1216 (1983).

6. *Musical Heights, Inc.*, 40 Rad. Reg.2d 1016 (1977). *Communico Oceanic Corp.*, 55 FCC 2d 733 (1975). *Greater Indianapolis Broadcasting Company, Inc.*, 44 FCC 2d 599 (1973). 47 C.F.R. § 73.1216 (1983).

7. *Honeyradio, Inc.*, 69 FCC 2d 833 (1978). *T/R, Inc.*, 38 Rad. Reg. 2d 1310 (1976). *Greater Indianapolis Broadcasting Company, Inc.*, 44 FCC 2d 599 (1973). *False, Misleading or Deceptive Advertising*, 40 FCC 125 (1961).

8. *Baron Radio, Inc.*, 25 Rad. Reg. 2d 1125 (1972). *In Re Public Notice Concerning Failure of Broadcast Licensees to Conduct Contests Fairly*, 45 FCC 2d 1056 (1974).

9. *KWK Radio, Inc.*, 35 FCC 561, 564 (1963).

10. *WMJX, Inc.*, 85 FCC 2d 251, 269 (1981). *Action Radio, Inc.*, 51 FCC 2d 803 (1975).

11. *SJR Communications, Inc.*, 45 FCC 2d 928 (1974).

12. *KOLOB Broadcasting Co.*, 36 FCC 2d 586 (1972). *Pacific and Southern Company, Inc.*, 44 FCC 2d 629 (1973).

13. *Independence Broadcasting Co., Inc.*, et al., 53 FCC 2d 1161 (1975). *Quiz Program Practices*, 14 FCC 2d 976 (1968). *National Broadcasting Co., Inc.*, 25 FCC 2d 106 (1970).

14. I.R.C. §§ 6041, 61.

15. 47 C.F.R. § 1.221 (1983).

16. *Folkways Broadcasting Co., Inc.*, et al., 48 FCC 2d 739 (1972).

17. *Ibid.*

18. *Metromedia, Inc.*, et al., 60 FCC 2d 1075, 1082–83 (1976); *Meredith Colon Johnston*, et al., 1 FCC 2d 720 (1965).

19. *Santa Rosa Broadcasting Co., Inc.*, 9 FCC 2d 644 (1967). *Oil Shale Broadcasting Company*, 68 FCC 2d 517 (1978). *Colonial Broadcasting Co.*, 44 Rad. Reg. 2d 1191 (1978). *Lawrence County Broadcasting Corp.*, 45 FCC 2d 881 (1974). *Qualitron Aero, Inc.*, 25 Rad. Reg. 2d 679 (1972). *WGOE, Inc.*, et al., 49 FCC 2d 327 (1974). 47 U.S.C. § 509 (1982).

20. *Melody Music, Inc.*, 2 FCC 2d 958 (1966). 47 U.S.C. § 509 (1982).

21. *Janus Broadcasting Company*, 78 FCC 2d 788 (1980). *Bremen Radio Co.*, 41 FCC 2d 595 (1973). *Kern County Broadcasting Co.*, 14 FCC 2d 292 (1968). *Eastern Broadcasting Corp.*, 8 FCC 2d 611 (1967). 47 U.S.C. § 509 (1982).

22. *Communico Oceanic Corp.*, 55 FCC 2d 733 (1975). *Randy Jay Broadcasting Company*, 64 FCC 2d 1121 (1977). *Weis Broadcasting Company*, 45 FCC 2d 536 (1974). 47 C.F.R. § 73.1216 (1983).

23. *Musical Heights, Inc.*, 40 Rad. Reg.2d 1016 (1977). *Henkin, Inc.*, 29 FCC 2d 40 (1971). *Eastern Broadcasting Corp.*, 14 FCC 2d 228 (1968). *WCHS-AM-TV Corp.*, 8 FCC 2d 608 (1967). 47 C.F.R. § 73.1216 (1983).

24. *LaFiesta Broadcasting, Inc.*, 59 FCC 2d 1175 (1976). *Bucks County Radio News, Inc.*, 61 FCC 2d 1091 (1976). *Radio Chesapeake, Inc.*, 29 Rad. Reg. 2d 1371 (1974). *In Re Public Notice Concerning Failure of Broadcast Licensees to Conduct Contests Fairly*, 45 FCC 2d 1056 (1974).

25. *Fox River Communications, Inc.*, 45 FCC 2d 1081 (1974). *In Re Public Notice Concerning Failure of Broadcast Licensees to Conduct Contests Fairly*, 45 FCC 2d 1056 (1974).

26. *In Re Public Notice Concerning Failure of Broadcast Licensees to Conduct Contests Fairly*, 45 FCC 2d 1056 (1974).

27. *WMJX, Inc.*, 85 FCC 2d 251, 273 (1981). *CBS, Inc., Tennis Match*, 67 FCC 2d 969 (1978). *Weis Broadcasting Company*, 45 FCC 2d 536 (1974).

28. *Fox River Communications, Inc.*, 45 FCC 2d 1081 (1974).

29. *Weirum v. RKO General, Inc.*, 539 P.2d 36 (Calif. 1975).

30. 47 C.F.R. § 73.1206 (1983).

31. 18 U.S.C. § 1304 (1982). 47 C.F.R. § 73.1211 (1983).

32. *Walton Broadcasting, Inc.*, 78 FCC 2d 857 (1980).

33. *Action Radio, Inc.*, 51 FCC 2d 803 (1975). *Honeyradio, Inc.*, 69 FCC 2d 833 (1978). *Public Notice Re Contests and Promotions Which Adversely Affect the Public Interest*, 2 FCC 2d 464 (1966).

34. *WGOE, Inc.*, et al., 49 FCC 2d 327 (1974). *National Broadcasting Co., Inc.*, 25 FCC 2d 106 (1970).

35. *CBS, Inc.*, 69 FCC 2d 1082 (1978).

36. *Belk Broadcasting Co. of Florida, Inc.*, 42 FCC 2d 844 (1973).

37. *CBS, Inc.*, 69 FCC 2d 1082 (1978).

38. *Channel 20, Incorporated*, 43 FCC 2d 1075 (1973).

39. *Folkways Broadcasting Co., Inc.*, et al., 48 FCC 2d 739 (1972).

40. *Ibid.*

41. *Greater Indianapolis Broadcasting Company, Inc.*, 44 FCC 2d 599 (1973). *Honeyradio, Inc.*, 69 FCC 2d 833 (1978). *Centrum Corp.*, 36 Rad. Reg.2d 201 (1976).

42. *KWK Radio, Inc.*, 34 FCC 1039, 1042 (1963). *Oil Shale Broadcasting Company*, 68 FCC 2d 517 (1978). *Walton Broadcasting, Inc.*, 78 FCC 2d 857 (1980). *Bremen Radio Co.*, 41 FCC 2d 595, 596 (1973). *Kern County Broadcasting Co.*, 14 FCC 2d 292 (1968).

43. *Henkin, Inc.*, 29 FCC 2d 40 (1971). *Eastern Broadcasting Corp.*, 14 FCC 2d 228 (1968). *Randy Jay Broadcasting Company*, 64 FCC 2d 1121 (1977).

44. *Independence Broadcasting Co., Inc.*, et al., 53 FCC 2d 1161 (1975). *Quiz Program Practices*, 14 FCC 2d 976 (1968).

45. *WMJX, Inc.*, 85 FCC 2d 251, 277 (1981).

46. *WMJX, Inc.*, 85 FCC 2d 251, 270 (1981).

47. *DAE Broadcasting Company*, 40 FCC 2d 107 (1973).

48. *V.I. Industries, Inc.*, 47 FCC 2d 271 (1974).

49. *Gaffney Broadcasting, Inc.*, 23 FCC 2d 912 (1970).

50. *Taft Broadcasting Company*, 18 FCC 2d 186 (1969).

51. *Thomasville Broadcasting Company*, 50 FCC 2d 919 (1975).

INDEX

INDEX OF STATIONS

West

East